Living with a
Shih Tzu

Edited by Josephine Johnson

BARRON'S

THE QUESTION OF GENDER
The "he" pronoun is used throughout this book in favor of the rather impersonal "it," but no gender bias is intended at all.

ACKNOWLEDGMENTS
Many thanks to Pauline Read for all her help, and Gloria Townsin of Redhall Shih Tzu (puppy chapter).

The publisher would also like to thank the following for help with photography: Rita Painter (Deenie) and Margaret Strangeland (Weatsom), Betty Williams (Crowvalley), and Ann Bradshaw (Jonarye).

First edition for the United States and Canada published
2002 by Barron's Educational Series, Inc.

© 2002 Ringpress Books

All inquiries should be addressed to:

Barron's Educational Series, Inc.
250 Wireless Boulevard
Hauppauge, NY 11788
http://www.barronseduc.com

International Standard Book Number 0-7641-5427-3

Library of Congress Catalog Card Number 2001088064

Printed in China through Printworks Int. Ltd.

9 8 7 6 5 4

CONTENTS

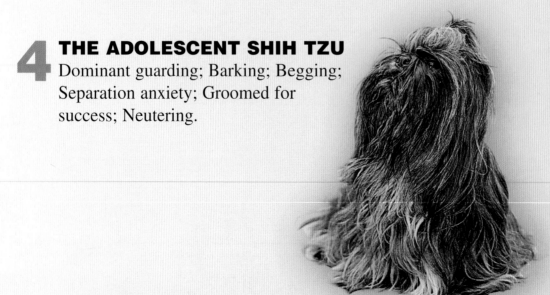

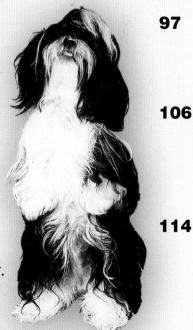

CHAPTER ONE

INTRODUCING THE SHIH TZU

Enigmatic and regal, with a glorious, long, thick coat, the Shih Tzu is the glamorous beauty of the canine world. Bred as a companion dog, the Shih Tzu makes an ideal pet, giving unconditional love and loyalty to his human family.

The haughty and disdainful expression that many Shih Tzus have perfected actually belies his true character – a fun-loving clown who provides lots of happiness, smiles and laughter wherever he goes.

Do not make the mistake of thinking the Shih Tzu is an easy-going lap dog, though. Strong-willed and assertive, this breed requires a no-nonsense owner who will give training, companionship, and leadership. Grooming is another essential commitment. The Shih Tzu's magnificent coat requires daily attention, and laborious grooming and bathing sessions. Even if the coat is trimmed short, daily brushing is still required (see Chapter Five).

If you lead a hectic life and cannot spare the time to care for a Shih Tzu properly, then it is better to choose a breed with an easy-maintenance coat and a less demanding character.

BUDDHIST BELIEFS

Categorized as a Chinese breed, the Shih Tzu's origins actually lie in Tibet, the remote, mountainous country on the Indian-Chinese border, which has shared a stormy relationship with China for centuries.

The religion of Tibet is Buddhism, which originally came from India. One of its chief tenets is that souls are reborn into another body (not necessarily human). This is seen as a process of learning until, eventually, the soul leads a perfect, spiritual, Buddhist life, and achieves nirvana. At this point, the soul does not need to be reborn, as there is nothing else for it to learn on the earth.

Early Tibetans believed that holy Buddhist monks who had transgressed were reincarnated as small, short-legged, hairy dogs – known as Ha-pa, meaning lap dog. Such dogs lived in Buddhist monasteries and were treated with great respect.

LION HEART

Inheriting the symbols of Indian Buddhism, the lion was a revered figure for the Tibetans, and it has a very close association with the Shih Tzu. Buddha Manjusri, the god of learning, is said to have a Ha-pa, which can turn into a lion for the Buddha to ride. A saddle marking on a Shih Tzu is still a highly prized characteristic for this reason.

Centuries ago, Tibetans would never have seen a lion, and so they developed their own highly stylized version. The small temple dogs were bred and groomed to resemble the Tibetan image of a lion, and, in fact, Shih Tzu Kou (as the breed was known) actually means Lion Dog.

The Lion Dog was highly revered by Tibetan Buddhists.

Of course, in the mountainous regions of Tibet, where the dogs would have been subjected to great extremes of temperature, a shaggy mane offered a practical purpose, as well as a symbolic one. Not only did the profuse coat keep the dogs warm, but, being lap dogs, they in turn kept their owners warm – as a canine hot-water bottle, the Shih Tzu is unsurpassed!

CHINESE WHISPERS

Tibet's relationship with China has always been stormy, and the country's history has featured many wars with and invasions by its powerful neighbor. Diplomacy between China's Emperors and Tibet's Dalai Lamas (spiritual leaders) was therefore a matter of great importance. Tactical marriages were arranged between royal Chinese princesses and Tibetan noblemen, and gifts of "tribute dogs" were often made to the Chinese Emperor. During the long span of the Manchu Dynasty (1643 to 1911), many dogs were presented to the Emperor; records show that three were received in 1650 alone.

The dogs were considered precious animals, and were not seen outside the Imperial Palace in Peking (now Beijing). They became a symbol of royalty, and for this reason "ordinary" people were not allowed to own them. Illegal ownership of a Shih Tzu was a crime that was punishable by death. However, it is now thought that the palace eunuchs, who were entrusted with the everyday care of the dogs, surreptitiously sold Shih Tzus (particularly those that were not suitable for breeding) for monetary gain.

The flat-faced, broad-headed features of the Pekingese, so admired by the Chinese, were reproduced in the Shih Tzu.

MADE IN CHINA

Although the Shih Tzu originated in Tibet, early Chinese breeding programs were responsible for developing the breed into what it is today. The Chinese have always had a penchant for flat-faced, broad-headed dogs (such as the Pekingese), and these features were reproduced in the Shih Tzu. Legend has it that the dogs' noses were broken with chopsticks while they were puppies, but selective breeding is more likely to have been responsible for this trait.

THE DOWAGER EMPRESS

Dowager Empress Tzu Hsi is an infamous character in Chinese history. One of the wives of Emperor Hsien Feng, the Dowager Empress ruled the country with Tzu An, another wife, when the Emperor died in 1861. The Empress's son, Tung Chih, succeeded his father, but, because he was only five years old, his mother and Tzu An acted as his protectors.

Tung Chih died in 1875, and the Empress's three-year-old nephew, Kuang Hsu, took over. Again, this gave the Empress the opportunity to rule through her juvenile relative, and her control of the country became absolute when her co-protectress, Tzu An, died shortly after Kuang Hsu's succession.

The Empress was said to be autocratic and cunning, and effectively ruled China for more than 50 years. Despite her full-time commitments to government, the Empress was devoted to her dogs.

Palace dogs were always treated to a life of luxury, sleeping on the finest silk and the most expensive rugs, but the Empress's dogs lived an excessively indulgent life. The Empress was

Interest waned in the Shih Tzu following the death of the Dowager Empress Tzu Hsi.

It is thought that the Pug was interbred with the Shih Tzu.

something of a sybarite, and enjoyed banquets where 150 different dishes were consumed, and she extended the same decadence to her canine companions. A palace dog, she decreed, was to be fed curlew's liver, shark fin, and quail breast, and its drink was to be antelope milk or "the tea that is brewed from the spring buds of a shrub that grows in the province of Hankow."

A great Pekingese breeder (she reputedly shared her life with more than 100 Pekes), the Empress also owned and bred Pugs. In 1908, the Dalai Lama gave the Empress a gift of a Shih Tzu. She was entranced by the breed, but, as she died the same year, little progress was made in breeding them. Sadly, after her death, royal interest in the Shih Tzu waned.

The eunuchs are believed to have continued to breed the dogs, but without the forethought and skill for which the Empress was famed. Some interbreeding between Pugs, Pekingese and Shih Tzus also took place, and it is thought that Shih Tzu blood was added to Peke lines in order to improve the coat. Crossbreeding was something the Empress abhorred, and she was always careful to keep the breeds separate.

REVOLUTION

Dog shows started to grow in popularity in the 1930s, but they came to an abrupt end in 1937 when the Japanese invaded China. Worse was yet to come. In 1949, the Chinese Communist party came to power. The Shih Tzu was one of the first victims of the new regime.

The Party considered it a waste to feed a dog when hungry peasants were in need of food, and so ordered the destruction of all canines. The Shih Tzu was one of the most despised of breeds because he had become a symbol of the Chinese royalty.

LEAVING CHINA

Fortunately, a few Westerners had managed to procure some Shih Tzus before the pogrom. Many puppies and adults died before reaching the West, and people concluded that the dogs must have been fed powdered glass by the sellers in a bid to keep Chinese dogs in China, where the breeders could still receive good money for the much-sought-after dogs. No Shih Tzus are believed to have survived the revolution in China.

Fortunately, a few Shih Tzus were taken from China, and the breed was established in Britain.

THE BREED IN BRITAIN

The first Shih Tzus were brought to the UK in 1930 by General and Mrs. Brownrigg. General Brownrigg (later Sir Douglas Brownrigg) served as Assistant Adjutant and Quartermaster General and bought a black-and-white bitch, who died in whelp. The Brownriggs acquired another black and white bitch, born in 1927, called Shussa. She was mated to a dog owned by Dr. Cenier, a Frenchman living in Peking. The Brownriggs adopted this dog, called Hibou, when Dr. Cenier returned to France.

A Miss Madelaine Hutchins, who also lived in China, acquired a male dog called Lung Fu Ssu, born in 1926, who accompanied her back to England in 1930, together with the Brownriggs' dogs. Shussa was mated to Hibou and whelped in quarantine. One of the puppies went to Miss Hutchins, two went to Lady Brownrigg's parents and another to one of Lady Brownrigg's friends in Scotland. In 1931, Lady Brownrigg returned to England and Shussa produced a second litter (from a mating to Lung Fu Ssu). Shussa's third litter (to Hibou) was born in 1932.

In the hands of enthusiastic and capable breeders, the popularity of the Shih Tzu grew steadily in the United Kingdom, but the outbreak of World War II halted most breeding programs and dog shows.

RETURN TO ROYALTY

Removed from the company of Chinese royalty, the Shih Tzu soon found favor with the British Royal Family. Mrs. Henrik Kauffman, married to the Danish Minister to China, was one of the first to export the Shih Tzu from China, taking three dogs back to Norway with her in 1932. One of the dogs, Leidza (born 1928) is the only dog known to have come from the Imperial Palace in Peking.

In 1933, Queen Maud of Norway presented Choo Choo to the Duchess of York (later Queen Elizabeth the Queen Mother).

Bred from two of Mrs. Kauffman's original Chinese Shih Tzu imports (Schander and Aidze), Choo Choo was a magnificent example of the breed, and soon became a much-loved pet in the royal household.

One of Choo Choo's male puppies was subsequently given by the Duchess as a present for Princess Margaret.

POST-WAR AND BEYOND

The first British Shih Tzu breed club was formed in 1934 and Mona Brownrigg was appointed secretary. The Shih Tzu was awarded Challenge Certificates (page 96) by the Kennel Club in 1940, but, because of the war, it wasn't until 1949 that the first Tzu Champion was created – Ta Chi of Taishan, granddaughter of Choo Choo, owned and bred by Mona Brownrigg.

Since then, the Shih Tzu has gone from strength to strength. Starting with just 183 registrations in 1939, it has soared to tenth position in the Kennel Club 2000 list of the nation's favorite breeds, notching up 3,782 registrations. The Shih Tzu's rise has been meteoric – and it doesn't look as if it is about to stop . . .

TO NORTH AMERICA

There was early confusion in America in the 1930s between the Shih Tzu and the Lhasa Apso, and the American Kennel Club is reported to have believed that the two were the same breed. The confusion resulted in some British and Scandinavian Shih Tzu exports to the United States being identified as Lhasa Apsos upon arrival. The Kennel Club intervened and pronounced the two breeds to be quite distinct.

Of course, the Lhasa Apso is closely related to the Shih Tzu, and there are strong similarities between the two, but the differences between them are also strong – notably, that the Shih Tzu has larger eyes, a shorter nose, and a wider muzzle than his Lhasa cousin.

The Shih Tzu (pictured above) bears a strong resemblance to the Lhasa Apso (below).

CROSSING BOUNDARIES

In 1952, the Shih Tzu world was hit by controversy when Freda Evans, a respected Pekingese breeder and relative newcomer to the Shih Tzu, sought permission from the Kennel Club to outcross one of her bitches to a Pekingese. Freda kept one bitch for breeding, who was bred back to a Shih Tzu. One bitch was kept from this subsequent litter and bred back again. The third-generation litter comprised six puppies, four of which were used for breeding.

Mrs. Evans's actions upset many breeders, mainly because the Shih Tzu Club was not consulted. However, some welcomed the move, as the breed gene pool was so small. Even including the Peke-cross, it is said that all Shih Tzus can be traced back to just 14 dogs.

Popularity Contest

The Shih Tzu grew in popularity after World War II. The breed caught the eye of army personnel based in the United Kingdom, who then returned to America with some of the

When the two breeds are clipped, it is easier to see the differences between the two. The Shih Tzu (pictured left) has larger eyes, a shorter nose, and a wider muzzle than his Lhasa cousin (right).

dogs, and the country's fascination with the breed grew from there.

The American Shih Tzu Club was established in 1957, and the AKC gave the Shih Tzu official recognition as a Toy breed in 1969. Choo Lang of Telota was the first dog to be registered.

The Shih Tzu is now one of the most popular of purebred dogs in the United States, boasting an impressive 37,599 registrations in 2000. With the current trend for small-breed dogs, better suited to modern, urban life, the Shih Tzu's popularity is assured.

A BREED APART

It comes as no surprise that the Shih Tzu is as popular as he is. For centuries, he has been bred to be the perfect companion – loving and lovable, and glamorous to boot. It is in his genes to enjoy human company and to give affection to his family.

Provided you are up to the challenge of caring for his needs properly, the Shih Tzu will certainly live up to all your expectations and prove himself to be a fun, charming, utterly irresistible housemate.

CHAPTER TWO

PUPPY POWER

Shih Tzu puppies are simply gorgeous – and that is part of their downfall. While you are deciding what breed is best for you (or, indeed, if a dog is the right pet for you), then you should do your very best to resist the Shih Tzu's soft, fluffy coat, the large, heart-melting eyes, and the comical, irresistible character.

Instead, think about the daily grooming, the twice-daily walks, the time needed to train the puppy, the sleepless nights, the veterinary costs (which can be hefty), the accidents around the house, the muddy paws on your carpet and your sofa, the mass of dog hair on your clothes, and the dog-care arrangements you will need to make whenever you go on vacation or leave the dog for more than four hours . . .

All of these factors should be seriously considered. The responsibility of owning a dog is tremendous, and it should be viewed as a long-term commitment – the Shih Tzu is a healthy breed that usually lives well into his mid- to late-teens.

Make sure you find out everything you can about the breed before deciding to take the plunge into ownership. Read books, search on the Internet, contact breed clubs, and attend

WELL GROOMED

The main reason for Shih Tzus ending up in rescue shelters is that people often under-estimate how much grooming the breed needs. The Shih Tzu needs grooming every day, and requires frequent bathing. Even if you take your dog to a professional groomer, you will still need to groom your Shih Tzu every day, and you will have to consider the cost of frequent grooming care. Do not choose this labor-intensive breed unless you are certain that you can spend the time attending to his daily grooming needs. See Chapter Five for more information.

shows where you can watch the breed in the show ring and talk to the exhibitors afterwards.

AVOIDING HEARTACHE

You should have no difficulty finding a Shih Tzu litter, but locating a well-bred, well-cared-for litter may be a little harder. Sadly, there are many unscrupulous breeders out there, who have exploited the breed's popularity, and who are producing hundreds of puppies from puppy farms/mills.

These puppies are usually from poor-quality parents, where the dams are relentlessly subjected to having litter after litter. The puppies will be raised in dirty environments (such as barns), where they will have little

The Shih Tzu is a labor-intensive breed, so think very carefully before making a commitment.

contact with people or the outside world. Their poor socialization, poor health and bad breeding does not prepare them for life as a pet. All too often, novice owners struggle with a snappy, nervous dog, and many end up with little option other than to give their dogs over to a rescue shelter. In some cases, the puppies die prematurely, causing a great deal of heartache (and expense) to their family.

All this could be avoided by taking the time to find an experienced, reputable breeder.

Storing Up Problems

Many puppy-farmed dogs end up in pet shops, and you are advised never to buy from such establishments. Not only are the animals likely to be of poor quality, and very badly socialized, but purchase from a store also encourages impulse-pet buying. Another important factor is that, although the staff may be fully conversant with animal care, they will not have the detailed knowledge and experience that a breeder has – and certainly not for every breed or species that they sell. A pet shop will never take back a four-year-old dog should your circumstances change, or answer a grooming query on a Sunday afternoon. A good breeder will accept lifelong responsibility for their dogs.

FINDING A GOOD BREEDER

The first step is to contact a breed club (your national kennel club will have details), and ask for reputable breeders in your area.

Be prepared to travel, as there may not be any breeders in your local area.

Contact the breeders and ask if they have a litter or if they are planning one for the near future. You may have to be patient, and wait for a few months, but your Shih Tzu puppy will be a member of your family for many years, so it is wise to find the best one you can.

If you are impressed by one of the breeders, you should arrange to visit them – even if there isn't yet a litter available. You will then be able to see their dogs and decide if you like the look of them.

• Are the dogs friendly?

• Do they look well-cared-for and healthy?

• Are the premises clean?

• Is the breeder friendly?

• Is the breeder asking you lots of questions about your circumstances, and how you propose to care for the puppy?

• Does the breeder provide a lifelong after-care service, so you can telephone and ask for advice at any point in the dog's life?

• Will the breeder take the dog back if necessary? A good breeder will be prepared to take the dog back if, in the future, you can no longer care for him.

• Meet the mother (or mother-to-be) of the puppies and assess her temperament and looks. Would you be happy for your puppy to turn out like her?

• Ask the breeder if there are any health problems in the line.

• Contact other experienced breeders (either at shows or through the breed club), and ask if the breeder you have chosen has a good reputation, and if their line is free from health

Assess the mother's temperament – it is a good indication of how the puppies will turn out.

problems and suspect temperaments.

If, at any stage of your visit, you have the slightest of doubts about the breeder or the dogs, then find another breeder. Choosing your Shih Tzu puppy is a very important decision, and you must feel 100 percent confident that you have the best puppy possible.

THE PERFECT PUPPY

Once you are happy that you have found the right breeder, then it is a case of waiting until a litter becomes available. During this time, you can get on with puppy-proofing your home and yard, and shopping for the new arrival (see pages 20-23).

When the puppies are old enough, the

breeder will invite you to visit the litter. The timing will depend on the age at which the breeder allows the puppies to leave for their new homes. Some breeders let the puppies go at eight weeks, others prefer to wait until the puppies are ten or eleven weeks, once the first vaccination has been given (see Chapter Nine). The majority of breeders will not allow you to view the litter until the pups are six weeks old.

At the first viewing you should again check the puppy's environment and meet the mother.

Next, check the puppies. Well-bred, healthy Shih Tzu puppies are clownish, outgoing, happy-go-lucky little souls. None of them should be nervous or shy, and they should all be eager to come forward to say hello. If there is a shy one, do not pick him out of pity. It is so

unusual to find a Shih Tzu with this type of temperament that such a puppy is best left to an experienced owner.

The breeder will tell you which puppies are still unclaimed, so, depending on the numbers in the litter (the average number is five), your choice might be limited, especially if you have stipulated that you want a particular sex or coat color.

MALE OR FEMALE?

Some people prefer male dogs, others prefer females, and some don't mind either way. With the Shih Tzu, the choice of sex is not as important as it is with other breeds, because, being a companion dog, the male is as loving as the female – in some cases, even more so. Some

The puppies should be lively and inquisitive, and they should be kept in clean surroundings.

males need more confident handling, so, if you are not naturally an assertive person, or you have never owned dogs before, a female may be a better choice.

If you already have a dog, then you may want to choose a puppy of the opposite sex. A male-female combination usually works very well, though you must ensure that one of the dogs at least is neutered to avoid any unwanted litters. If you choose a female, you will have to cope with her seasons, unless she is neutered. See Chapter Four for more information.

COLOR

The Shih Tzu has many coat colors, all of which are acceptable in the show ring. All the following colors can be as solid (whole) colors, or can be combined with white (parti-colored).

- Black
- Gray
- Blue (rare)
- Liver
- Brindle
- Silver
- Gold

You shouldn't really base your choice of puppy on coat color alone, as the Shih Tzu is famous for changing his color throughout his life. For example, a black-and-white dog with white skin will develop a lighter coat as he ages, eventually becoming gray-and-white. (A dog with darker, "blue" skin, however, will stay black-and-white.) A gold puppy could turn a distinct orange color.

Also, if you have a strong preference, you may have to wait a very long time before a puppy with your chosen color combination becomes available.

Shih Tzus come in a variety of colors, and the shade may change as the puppy matures.

SHOW PUPPY

If you would like a puppy that you can show, you should inform the breeder from the outset. In a litter, there may be only one puppy with show potential, and it is likely that the breeder will want to keep it. If there are two, and there are no other people interested in a show puppy, then you might be in luck.

A show-quality puppy is likely to be a natural show-off. Physically, he will look like a miniature adult. Read the Breed Standard (see Chapter Eight), and look at the puppy's construction. It is much easier to assess his skeletal conformation, as it will not be hidden by an abundant coat yet. The best advice is to be guided by the breeder, who will have a good eye for assessing puppies.

Do be warned, though – breeders are not fortune tellers. Although they can see which puppy has show potential, there is no guarantee that the potential will come to fruition as the Shih Tzu matures. Mouths and noses, in particular, can change in a matter of weeks,

It is very difficult to assess show potential in a young puppy.

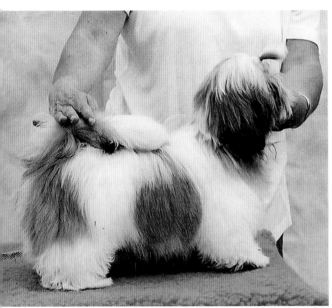

As the puppy gets bigger, it is easier to see what you are getting, but, beware, a youngster can go through many changes before reaching maturity.

rendering the dog completely unsuitable for the show ring. You will just have to acknowledge that the dog's show future is in the lap of the gods. If it happens, it happens. If it doesn't – well, you still have a fantastic friend and companion. See Chapter Six for more information on showing.

PRE-PUPPY PREPARATIONS

So you have finally picked your puppy. Now it's just a matter of waiting before you can go get him. The wait can seem like forever – but you can use this time productively, preparing for your new arrival.

Shopping List

There are a number of items you will need to purchase before bringing home the puppy. You were warned that puppies are expensive, and now you are about to put the theory to the test!

A Crate

These metal cages may look uninviting, but with some comfortable bedding and some fun, safe toys, your puppy will love his new den, and you will love it too – crates are invaluable when raising a puppy.

Buy the crate that will comfortably accommodate an adult Shih Tzu, as your dog may occasionally use the crate throughout his life. The right size should be around 24 inches long, 20 inches wide, and 22 inches high (57.5 cm x 48 cm x 53 cm). See page 42.

The crate can also be used instead of a car harness when your dog is travelling in a car, providing safe and secure accommodation.

Bedding

Fleecy veterinary bedding is the best type to buy. It is soft, warm, absorbent (in case of accidents) and usually machine-washable. Placed in a crate, such bedding instantly turns it into a cozy retreat for your puppy.

Whatever toys you buy, make sure they are of good quality – puppies have incredibly sharp teeth and can chew through soft plastic with ease. Squeakers can come loose and be swallowed, which can be fatal. Check your Shih Tzu's toys regularly, and replace them if they show any signs of damage.

Food

Ask the breeder what food you need to buy. It is advisable to feed the diet your puppy has been used to, in order to avoid stomach upsets (see page 24).

Bowls

Your Shih Tzu will need food and water bowls. There are lots on the market – plastic, stainless steel, or ceramic.

Each has advantages and disadvantages. Plastic is cheap and won't break, but scratches (and is chewable). Stainless steel will last forever, but makes noise if dropped, and some dogs can be spooked by their own reflections when eating. Ceramic bowls come in lots of attractive designs, are easy to keep clean, but can break.

Tip: generally, Shih Tzus do not like deep bowls so use a shallow one.

Collar and Lead

Your puppy's collar and lead should be chosen with care. Don't just opt for the prettiest one you see. Comfort is the main priority, or your Shih Tzu will resent wearing a collar and lead.

Remember also that, when your puppy's coat

It is a good idea to prepare your home and yard before your puppy arrives home.

Baby Gate

An adjustable baby gate (also known as a pressure gate) is a very useful piece of equipment in a puppy household. Fitted securely to restrict the puppy's access, the gate can be used to stop the puppy going outside, upstairs, downstairs, or anywhere else he shouldn't be.

Toys

All puppies are playful, but Shih Tzu pups are more playful than most. Squeaky toys and rope toys are particularly enjoyed, but they will play with virtually anything – an old knotted sock or a crumpled ball of newspaper will be equally acceptable.

grows, some collars will be unsuitable. Wide, heavy collars are not ideal, nor are collars with metal buckles which will tangle the coat.

Soft, webbed, nylon collars which clip together are popular with Shih Tzu owners, and are quick and easy to put on and take off.

A lead will also be required; make sure it is not too heavy – ideally, you don't want your puppy even to know he is wearing it. The lead must also be comfortable for you, so test a few before making your decision.

An identity tag should also be purchased. Many shops provide an in-house engraving service where the tag can be etched with your contact details.

Grooming Equipment

Many breeders use a baby hairbrush for a Shih Tzu's first brush. To begin with, use a small good-quality bristle brush. When the dog has a longer coat, a pin brush is required, but it should be used gently as it can hurt the dog and damage the coat. A soft slicker brush is needed when the coat changes after female's first season or around the age of one year for males.

A comb is essential, as a brush will never remove all the tangles. A comb which is wide-toothed at one end and narrow-toothed at the other is ideal. You will also need a moustache comb for when your Shih Tzu develops his facial furnishings. These combs are smaller versions of the comb described above.

Puppy-Proofing

Before bringing home your Shih Tzu puppy,

The inquisitive Shih Tzu will investigate everything, so make sure your house is 100 percent safe.

you must make sure that your house and yard are completely safe. If you have never had a puppy before, do not underestimate their powers of destruction! Shih Tzu pups may look sweet and innocent, but they can chew through most substances known to man, they have a great talent for urinating on "dry-clean only" garments, and vases and ornaments seem to throw themselves off shelves and tables the moment a Shih Tzu puppy walks into a room. Puppy-proof your home while you still have a home to proof!

Puppy-proofing isn't just about protecting your household objects from damage; more importantly, it ensures your Shih Tzu remains safe from all domestic dangers. It only takes a curious puppy to chew through an electrical wire, to swallow a sewing needle, or to eat toxic slug pellets and tragedy can strike.

Be safe, not sorry. Crawl around your house on your hands and knees and see your home from a puppy's perspective. Remove overhanging tablecloths that he can pull, make sure he cannot reach any electrical cables, put shoes away in your closet, remove any ornaments that can be knocked over, and put houseplants safely out of reach (many are poisonous, and tall plants on the floor will encourage male dogs to lift their leg). All fireplaces should be fitted with secure guards.

Then turn your attention to the yard. Shih Tzus can crawl through the tiniest of spaces, so check that there are no gaps in or under your fencing. Be warned that a Shih Tzu can overcome most obstacles when he sets his mind to it, so make sure your dog cannot dig his way out under fences or climb his way over the top. Fences should be fairly high (4 feet/1.3m is ideal), with good, deep foundations.

If you have a garden pond or a pool, make sure it is fenced off or securely covered.

If you have a garden pond or swimming pool, make sure it is fenced off so your Shih Tzu cannot get near it. It is also worth checking with a garden center that your plants are not toxic to dogs. Remove all wild toadstools or mushrooms for the same reason. Make sure that any garden chemicals you use are dog-friendly, or ensure that your Shih Tzu never comes into contact with them – many types of weed killer, slug pellets, and insecticide can be fatal if ingested.

Vetting Veterinarians
Before you bring your puppy, home register with a local veterinary practice. Do not choose one randomly from a telephone directory – your relationship with your dog's doctor is an important one, and you should find the most suitable and not just the most convenient. Perhaps your dog-owning friends or family can recommend some good veterinarians in your area. When you contact the veterinarians, ask the following questions.

- What hours are they open?
- Do you have to wait long for an appointment?
- Do they have any testing equipment on site?
- What is their policy on home visits?
- What off-hour services are available?
- Does the practice offer alternative therapies (if this is important to you)?
- Has anyone at the practice ever owned a Shih Tzu?

Make an appointment to look around the clinic and to talk to the staff, who will be more than happy to answer any questions.

Once you have found a veterinarian you are happy with, make an appointment for the day after you acquire your puppy. The veterinarian can then perform a health-check and arrange your Shih Tzu's vaccination and worming schedule. It is worth also discussing pet insurance with your vet, who will have details of various options.

Take the opportunity to discuss permanent identification with your vet. Tattooing is used in many locations, but can be unsightly, and many owners are now opting to have their dogs microchipped. This involves a small chip, the size of a large grain of rice, being injected between the shoulder blades. When scanned with a reader (which veterinarians, dog wardens and rescue centers all have access to), the microchip will reveal a unique number which corresponds to your contact details. These details can be updated if you move. It ensures that your dog can be traced back to you in the event of losing his identification tag.

ACQUIRING THE PUPPY

Arrange to acquire your Shih Tzu in the morning. This will give you the chance to travel home and settle the puppy into his new home well before bedtime. If you can, arrange for a friend to accompany you to the breeder. This will enable one of you to hold the puppy securely on your lap while the other drives.

Ask the breeder to give you a small article or toy to take with you, to help settle your puppy into his new home.

Put a soft towel on your lap in case of accidents, and make sure you take some water and a bowl with you so that your puppy can have a drink if it is hot, in case you get stuck in traffic or break down. Make sure there is ample shade and ventilation in the car, so that the puppy does not overheat.

If you need to stop on the journey, remember not to allow your puppy to come into contact with other dogs or places where other dogs may have been. Until he has finished his course of puppy vaccinations, he will be in danger of contracting very serious diseases (Chapter Nine).

If you can't find anyone who can travel with you, then you will have to place the puppy in a crate (page 42) in the back of the car. Under no circumstances let the puppy loose in the car – it would be dangerous for you both.

HOME AT LAST

When you arrive home, take your Shih Tzu puppy out to your yard to stretch his legs, relieve himself (page 36), and sniff about. If you already have a dog, let him out to meet the puppy (page 33).

FEEDING

The pet food industry is a large one, and there are numerous manufacturers producing many different types of food – canned meat and biscuits, complete food, and frozen meat meals. Some people prefer to feed fresh meat and vegetables, but it is vital that the dog is given the right quantity of the many vitamins and minerals he requires to be healthy. Remember – nutrition is an exact science, with overdosage being as dangerous as underdosage.

To begin with, feed your Shih Tzu puppy whatever the breeder recommends. He or she will have considerable experience in feeding Shih Tzus and will have probably tried many of the different types of food on the market, before finding what works best.

When you go to get the puppy, the breeder should provide you with a diet sheet, outlining what you should feed, how much, and when. Follow this to the letter. A sudden change in diet, particularly if combined with a change in all the puppy's other routines, can result in stomach upsets.

When you first get your puppy, he will probably be on four meals a day, and this can be reduced to three meals within a couple of weeks of bringing him home. Your puppy will gradually lose interest in one of his meals, which can be phased out altogether, increasing the size of the other three feedings.

By the time the pup is around six months old, he should be weaned on to two meals a day – breakfast and supper. A few owners prefer to cut this down further to one meal a day, but Shih Tzus generally prefer two meals.

Changing the Menu

If you would like to change your Shih Tzu puppy's food (perhaps you are having difficulty getting hold of the recommended brand, or it does not seem to agree with your puppy), consult the breeder or your veterinarian, who may be able to recommend another food to you.

REST AND RELAXATION

Puppies need lots of sleep, so remember to provide frequent nap breaks throughout the day. Don't expect your puppy to cope with the journey home, meeting the resident pets and the rest of the family, investigating his new home, and meeting all your friends and neighbors all on the same day.

Take things slowly – you have plenty of time to show off your adorable puppy, so don't overwhelm your Shih Tzu on the first day. If he is overtired, he will become irritable, which is not the best way to start your new life together.

As a general guide, plan for your puppy to catch up on his beauty sleep every couple of hours. You need to groom your Shih Tzu every day, and you will have to consider the cost of frequent grooming care. Do not choose this labor-intensive breed unless you are certain that you can spend the time attending to his daily grooming needs. See pages 68-74 for more information.

Give your puppy a chance to explore the yard.

Gradually introduce some of the new food to the puppy's existing diet. Over the course of a week, add more of the new food and less of the former food, until a complete replacement has been made.

Fussy Eaters

Shih Tzus, in common with other small-breed dogs, have a reputation for being fussy eaters. However, many problems can be prevented by dealing with your dog's eating habits in the right way from the very start.

- When you put food down for your Shih Tzu, leave it down for five minutes and then remove it – whether it is eaten or not. Your puppy will soon learn to eat his food when you put his bowl down.
- If your puppy leaves his food, never replace it with something else. This teaches your puppy

Do not attempt to change your puppy's diet until he has settled.

that he can pick and choose. Never replace his ordinary food with fresh fish, chicken or something equally mouthwatering, or your puppy will learn that the longer he fasts, the better the eventual rewards!

- If your puppy loses his appetite for more than 24 hours, consult your veterinarian. Once it is established that stubbornness and opportunism are the causes, and not ill health, then stick to your guns, however tempting it is to give in. Your puppy will soon learn that he cannot call the shots.

EXERCISING

The Shih Tzu may be small, but what he lacks in size, he more than makes up for in terms of energy. This does not mean he needs two half-hour route marches every day. As a growing puppy, the Shih Tzu's skeleton and joints should not be put under undue pressure. That means no climbing – or falling down – the stairs, no leaping out of the car, and no jumping off high furniture.

Until he is fully inoculated, play in the yard should provide all the exercise the puppy needs. Never overtire the puppy, something which is easily done, especially if you have children. The Shih Tzu loves fun, and will not stop if there is a game to play. He will go on and on and on until he is exhausted. Do your puppy's thinking for him. When you think he's enjoyed enough high-energy play, then shift down a gear to gentle play or cuddles, and then perhaps a nap in his crate.

Once your Shih Tzu is able to go out in

To begin with, your puppy will get all the exercise he needs playing in the yard.

public places, start off with just a few minutes of lead-walking (page 50) and about 10 minutes running around a park. Gradually extend the length of his exercise period as he grows. See page 65 for details of adult exercise requirements.

PLAY

Puppies love to play. As with all juvenile creatures, play offers opportunities for them to develop life skills necessary for adulthood, including social interaction. A Shih Tzu puppy is more than capable of amusing himself – he will play with almost anything he can lay his paws on – but just because he can, doesn't mean he should.

Yes, it's fine to give your puppy a safe toy and let him entertain himself while you peel the potatoes or read the paper. But make sure you set time aside for play sessions together. Shih Tzus are companion dogs, and it is important to spend quality time with your puppy. You will both have a great deal of fun, and it serves as a good bonding experience.

FIRST NIGHT

Before settling your Shih Tzu into his crate for the night, take him outside to relieve himself, avoiding any excitement or play. Make sure he has bedding in his crate, and some safe toys to play with or chew. Place some newspapers at the front end of the crate in case your puppy needs

It's not easy, but try to harden your heart, and give your pup a chance to settle.

to relieve himself in the night (the ability to control his bladder will improve as he ages). Then put your puppy in his crate, switch on a radio in the room and set it to a low volume, say goodnight and leave.

Your Shih Tzu may nod off immediately, remain in a deep sleep all night, and awake at the same time you do the next morning. But this is very, very unlikely! In all probability, he will howl, cry, and bark pitifully for hours and hours on end. The familiar item from home your breeder gave you (page 24) may help him to settle a little more easily.

Annoying though it may be (after three nights, your sanity will begin to suffer), you shouldn't be angry with your puppy – his behavior is entirely understandable. Until now, your sociable Shih Tzu has never been alone. He has spent the first weeks with his mother,

littermates, breeder and family, and you have been with him all day in his new home. Now he is utterly alone, in a quiet, dark, unfamiliar place with strange sounds and smells and no one to cuddle up to.

Tempting though it is to go to your puppy, or to bring him into bed with you, be warned that this sets a dangerous precedent. Your puppy will probably settle down right away, so the next night when he cries, you will crack again . . . and again . . . and again. This is a clear case of the puppy training you – when you should be training the puppy! Soon, it is the routine that the puppy sleeps with you. This is fine if you want your dog to share your bed every night for the next 15 or so years, but, if you would prefer to enjoy more room in your bed, set the boundaries from the very start and stick to them. (A good compromise would be to locate the puppy's crate *near* your bed. That way, everyone stays happy.)

Earplugs and willpower are invaluable for coping with your puppy's first week. If you remain strong and resist returning to him, every night will become easier, and he will be sleeping through the night in no time at all.

FELINE FADS

Like cats, many Shih Tzus like to make their own beds before lying down. They will scramble their bedding into what appears a big mess (some even making a raised pillow effect on which to lay their head!), before settling. Don't be surprised – this is normal behavior for a Shih Tzu!

CHAPTER THREE

EARLY LESSONS

Once you have settled your Shih Tzu into his new home, you can start on his training and socialization program. Never think that your Shih Tzu puppy is too young to learn – the younger he is, the better. Puppies exude confidence, and soak up experiences like a sponge. It is much better that your puppy learns house rules, good manners and early obedience exercises as soon as possible to get a really valuable head start in life.

CHILDISH BEHAVIOR

Many breeders will place a puppy in a family with well-behaved, older children, but the majority will not allow their dogs to go to a home where very young children (under school age) are present. The Shih Tzu may look like a child's cute, cuddly toy, but he is not. Small children can accidentally drop a puppy or tread on him, and it simply isn't fair to subject a living creature to this kind of behavior.

It is vital that children are taught how to behave around the puppy, well before he arrives home, and that they are always supervised when together with your Shih Tzu. Here are some basic rules:

- Teasing is never allowed.
- All play must be gentle.
- Running near the puppy is forbidden.
- The puppy can only be picked up if the child is seated on the floor.
- The puppy must not be disturbed if he is sleeping.

You should also agree what house rules the puppy should follow, and make sure everyone in the family knows them. These rules may include some of the following. Every home is different – discuss what rules are important to you, then stick to them.

- Never feed the puppy from the table (page 57).
- If the puppy is not allowed on the beds or furniture (which is advisable in the Shih Tzu),

then everyone should make sure the rule is implemented.

• Always make sure doors, gates, and windows that the puppy can reach are closed securely so the puppy can't come to any harm.

WHO'S BOSS?

Despite his diminutive size and angelic good looks, the Shih Tzu can become a bit of a power freak if he does not understand, from the very beginning, his status in the family pack (see Chapter Four).

It is important that your Shih Tzu grows up to respect children, rather than believing he is superior to them. It is therefore vital to involve children in the puppy's early training. If you do not have any children of your own, beg, borrow or steal them (okay, maybe not steal). Enlist the help of nieces, nephews, grandchildren, or the children of friends or neighbors.

Most children will jump at the chance of spending time with a puppy – especially one as gorgeous as the Shih Tzu.

Bowled Over

Many dogs can become possessive over their food. It is understandable if you consider that, despite thousands of years of domestication, the dog still has many of the same instincts that he had when he lived in the wild. Food means the difference between life and death. You can't blame your Shih Tzu for not realizing that you will provide ample food for the rest of his life – if he feels insecure or wants to assert his dominance over those around him, he will feel

Generally, Shih Tzus are better suited to living in a family with older children.

justified in guarding his food, fearful that it may be stolen.

Your puppy must be told right from the start, that all people, regardless of their age, size, or sex, are allowed to go near his bowl. The best way of teaching him this rule is to remove his insecurity and to reward him for allowing his bowl to be taken.

• When you feed your Shih Tzu one of his meals, put in only half of the allocation and then give him the bowl.

• Just before he finishes, while he is still eating, pick up the bowl and put in the remaining half of the meal.

Adding a treat to the food will ensure that the puppy does not become possessive over his meal.

Once your puppy is used to this routine, it's time to introduce the help of a well-behaved child.

- When the puppy is eating one of his meals, ask the child to put a really tasty treat into the bowl. Choose your puppy's favorite food, be it chicken, cheese or liver.
- It won't take your shrewd Shih Tzu very long to realize that child plus bowl equals tasty treat.
- As the puppy grows, use this exercise periodically with different members of the family, to remind him that there is no reason to be possessive about food.

Play Away

The same type of exercise should be used to prevent the puppy becoming possessive of his toys.

- Give your Shih Tzu a toy to play with.
- Take the toy, then give him a food treat and lots of praise before giving the toy back to him.
- If he has the toy in his mouth, very gently remove it, while giving the command "Give." Then reward him, as before.
- Repeat this three or four times a day initially. All family members should be involved so that your puppy learns to surrender his possessions to whoever asks.
- Always end the exercise with you having possession of the toy (if the puppy sees himself as the "victor," it can encourage dominance – see pages 53-55).
- As before, the training can be reduced as the puppy gets older, but a weekly refresher session will prove useful.

It is important that both children and puppies learn to respect each other.

Bite Inhibition

Like human babies, puppies explore with their mouths, and it is natural that your Shih Tzu puppy will want to mouth your hand or clothing. As soon as he does, he must be shown that this is inappropriate as teeth should never come into contact with people.

As with all areas of training, solidarity is essential. Everyone the puppy encounters – family, friends, and neighbors – must behave in the same way if the puppy mouths them.

Every time the puppy mouths, yelp in a high-pitched squeak (as another puppy would), turn away from your Shih Tzu and ignore him. This should be done whether the puppy hurts you or not.

Puppies hate to be ignored, especially prima donna Shih Tzu puppies that adore being the center of attention. Your puppy will soon learn that mouthing or biting is not an option if he is to win friends and influence people.

Learning Together

Training engenders respect – it is a way for you and your Shih Tzu to spend quality time together, and to work as a team. It is important, therefore, that all family members are involved in the puppy's training from the very start. Once you have taught the puppy the basic obedience exercises (pages 46-49), a child (or, ideally, various children), should practice the exercises with the puppy.

CANINE COMPANIONS

If you already have a resident dog, it is much better if the puppy is introduced outside rather

Shih Tzus are sociable dogs, and, if you are tactful in the early stages, a group of dogs will live in harmony.

than in your house where there are more territorial issues at stake.

Assuming your adult dog is good with pets (otherwise, why are you getting a puppy?), there shouldn't be any problems with the canine introductions. Shih Tzu puppies are very confident and friendly, even with dogs much bigger than themselves, so it is unlikely that your Shih Tzu will be frightened or aggressive.

The most important rule for the first meeting is to remain calm. Dogs are excellent at picking up on an owner's anxiety, and they will become nervous and excitable if they think that you are tense. Let the dogs approach each other (off-leash) in their own time. If the older dog grumbles at the puppy, don't intervene – it is doggie language for "Look, kiddo, this is my turf; you're welcome to stay, but on my terms, okay? Follow my rules, don't tread on my toes, and we'll get along just fine."

If you intervene, or, worse still, reprimand your adult dog, you will be telling them that the puppy is senior to the older dog in the family hierarchy. This can cause endless problems. Dogs are great communicators. Let them work out their status between themselves. Whoever comes out naturally as top dog (in 99 percent of cases, the older dog), respect their decision, and reinforce the hierarchy, feeding the top dog first and so on. For more information on hierarchy, see Chapter Four.

Remember to set aside quality time with your older dog so he still feels loved, and make sure he is given an option to escape from the puppy (such as a puppy-free room).

FELINE-FRIENDLY

The Shih Tzu is a very cat-friendly breed, provided he is raised with cats. If you want a cat-friendly puppy, find a breeder that has house cats, so the puppy will grow up to be calm and well behaved around them.

If you are planning to introduce a new Shih Tzu puppy to your resident cat, then you must first assess whether your cat is dog-friendly. If she is terrified of dogs, then you must think seriously about whether it is fair to bring a puppy home. Cornered cats will lash out with their claws, and you do not want to be forever worrying about your dog receiving eye injuries from your irate or anxious cat. In such circumstances, it would be kinder to put your puppy plans on hold until you can bring in a puppy-friendly kitten and start fresh.

If your cat is fully dog-proof, great care must still be taken to avoid jealousy and resentment between the animals. Remember also that, however much we would like to deny the fact, pets often reflect their owners' personalities. Generally, nervous, excitable people end up with nervous, excitable pets, so be as calm and laid-back as you can.

- For the very first meeting, put the puppy in his crate (pages 20, 42), and let kitty approach in her own time to sniff out the newcomer.

- Once your cat has investigated the puppy, and seems calm, then you can release him. At the same time, make a big fuss over your cat, stroking her and talking calmly to reassure her. This will make her realize that she is still

THE CAT'S WHISKERS

Geraldine Moston (Hiona Shih Tzus) from Stoke-on-Trent, Staffordshire, England not only has her work cut out with six Shih Tzus to care for, but she also has three long-haired Persian cats too. Far from being a center of chaos, however, Geraldine's home is peace personified.

"I love long hair and short noses – which is probably why I never got married!" laughs Geraldine. "My cats and dogs all get along well together – they have never known anything different. Because my cats are house cats, the dogs see them all the time, and they have never even thought of chasing them.

"When I breed a litter, the cats all get very interested in the puppies and lick their faces to clean away the food. I expect the puppies think they are cats most of the time. The puppies have their own litter tray (filled with shredded newspaper) in the early days too, which helps with their house-training. They just watch the cats and copy them.

"There are lots of similarities between Shih Tzus and cats. I think the Shih Tzu is 95 percent cat – they must be related in some way. Shih Tzu puppies look quite feline; they have what appears to be whiskers, until the face furnishings grow downwards. Shih Tzu adults play like cats, using their paws to move toys, which many dog breeds don't do. And, like cats, Shih Tzus are very regal and proud.

"I have even had Shih Tzus that stalk like cats – both of them were golden (it seems different colors have different traits). Kate would stalk blackbirds and bring them into the house. She was very gentle and didn't harm them – they would just be a bit soggy and stunned.

"Tussah, also gold-colored, jumps like a cat – leaping up on to high furniture and sleeping curled up on the back of a chair as a cat would. She also washes the cats' faces and ears, something they do not seem to mind. In fact, Shih Tzus self-groom like cats, and furballs are a problem in the breed.

DOMESTIC HARMONY

"My dogs and cats eat together, which is a sociable, bonding experience, reaffirming and harmonizing their relationships with each other. They are groomed all together, too, which is another bonding routine. Plus, we all sleep together. Every night, I share my bed with two Shih Tzus and three Persians. One of my females, Jing, had a litter recently. When I went to bed the first night, one by one she brought all the puppies up to my bed. She wanted us all to be together! When I took all the puppies back to the whelping box, Jing gave me a filthy look. Drusilla, one of my Persians, has done the same with her litter. They all seem to think we should sleep together at night . . ."

Toffee the Shih Tzu with Persian cats Portia (blue) and Claudia (cream).

loved, and that, in the family hierarchy, she is superior to the newcomer.

- Your cat's curiosity will probably get the better of her, and she won't be able to resist going up to meet the puppy. Remain calm, and let them sniff each other. If the puppy gets too boisterous, your cat will probably spit and hiss – and most pups don't need telling twice. Always make sure that your cat can jump up on something to escape the puppy if necessary.
- Never leave the cat and Shih Tzu alone unsupervised until you are absolutely certain that they can be trusted together. Your puppy should be kept in his crate, safely out of harm's way, whenever you are unable to watch him.

FIRST LESSONS

HOUSE-TRAINING
House-training a puppy is not rocket science – follow some simple rules and you will never have to reach for the mop and bucket again.

Routine
- Allocate a particular spot in your yard which will become your puppy's toileting area.
- Take him to this spot frequently throughout the day (see box, this page).
- Be patient. If he doesn't perform immediately, wait until he does.
- If, after ten minutes, your Shih Tzu has failed to perform, take him inside and try again half an hour later.

- As soon as your puppy relieves himself, say "Be clean," "Get busy" or whatever command you plan to use.
- Give lots of praise, and play together for a few minutes afterwards. Do not return indoors immediately, or your puppy will learn to keep his legs crossed in order to avoid going inside.
- Avoiding accidents is a good way to train. When you can't watch the puppy, confine him to a crate.

Be Vigilant
Watch your puppy closely. If he starts looking for a corner to hide in, starts sniffing the ground, circling, or squatting, you must act quickly to avoid an accident. Clap your hands to

---

REGULAR ROUTINE

Take your puppy outside at the following times.

- As soon as he wakes up.
- Before and after periods of exercise or excitement (i.e. meeting new people, play and so on).
- After eating.
- Before he has a nap or goes to bed for the night.
- Every two hours.

This list might seem excessive, but you can never take your puppy outside too often. The more opportunities you provide him with to relieve himself, the less likely he is to have an accident. If you can avoid accidents in the house, your puppy will soon understand that he relieves himself outside.

If you stick to a routine, your puppy will soon learn to be clean in the house.

startle him (he'll stop what he's doing immediately) and then encourage him outside in a happy, excited way.

Accidents Happen

Despite your best efforts, there are bound to be times when your puppy has an occasional accident. Annoying though it is, it is a fact of raising a puppy, so just clean it up and resolve to be extra-vigilant to prevent it happening again.

It is hard to stop yourself getting mad at the puppy, but this will certainly not help matters. He won't be able to link the cause (which could have appeared several hours ago) with the effect. Your pup will think you are shouting because he is playing with a ball – or whatever he is doing when you discover his mishap – and will become thoroughly confused.

DIRTY HABITS

Some puppies and a few adult dogs eat their own – or other dogs' – feces. Coprophagy is something of a taboo subject among pet owners, with many people being too embarrassed to confess their puppy's bad habit. Sadly, the Shih Tzu breed has its fair share of culprits.

The best way of dealing with the problem is to prevent it.

- As soon as your puppy relieves himself, clean it up.
- When walking in a public area, keep a close eye on your Shih Tzu. If you notice that he is sniffing – and about to eat – something he shouldn't, call him to you at once and give him a much more tasty treat for obeying. (See page 46 for good recall.) Alternatively, you can distract your dog by throwing on the ground some metal training discs or a can with a couple of pebbles inside.
- If the appeal is really too much for him and he refuses to come to you, call upon a professional dog trainer or behaviorist. It is important that your puppy's antisocial behavior is corrected before it becomes habitual.

NAME GAME

Naming a puppy is either incredibly easy or incredibly difficult! Some puppies seem to inspire the right name instantly, while others are known as "puppy" for weeks while the family has endless meetings to decide on something suitable. Try to choose a name as quickly as possible, so that your puppy can learn his name from the start – otherwise, just as he gets used to "puppy," he will have to relearn his proper name.

Tip: choose something short and snappy. Calling your puppy an unusual Tibetan name may seem a clever idea, but "Manjusri, Come!" doesn't exactly roll off the tongue with ease.

GROOMING

The Shih Tzu puppy has a coat that is relatively easy to care for – provided it is groomed regularly. You should get into good grooming habits while the puppy is still young, so you both become accustomed to the routine. Brush your Shih Tzu puppy at the end of every walk, to remove any debris from the coat and set aside a few minutes at the same time every day for another grooming session.

The breeder will probably have provided you with details of how to manage the coat, but here are some basic guidelines.

Early Sessions

• Use a soft bristle brush initially, and, while the puppy is on your lap, stroke him all over with the brush.
• Gently roll him on to his back to groom his underside. Carefully brush his tail.
• All the time you are grooming him, talk to him calmly and praise him for being good.
• Give him a treat at the end of the session as a reward. You must show your puppy that grooming is an enjoyable experience – after all, it will feature as a major part of the rest of his life.
• If your puppy attempts to bite, or play with,

The long-haired Shih Tzu must learn to accept grooming and handling.

the brush, tell him "No" firmly, and continue. Never stop the session because your Shih Tzu demands it – this will encourage him to misbehave. It goes without saying that the brush should never be used to admonish the puppy.
• Keep the initial sessions very short (five minutes should suffice), and make sure the puppy is groomed gently. If grooming is painful for him, he will learn to hate it and will become difficult to handle.
• As the coat grows, gradually lengthen the time of your grooming sessions, and use a firmer bristle brush. Finish off by combing the puppy through with a medium-toothed comb, then play together to reward the puppy for his good behavior.

Stand

Once your Shih Tzu is used to being handled all over, you should get him accustomed to standing on a table to be groomed. Choose where you want to groom your puppy, and try not to change the location – you want your puppy to associate the spot with what is expected of him.

- Place your puppy on the table, with all your equipment at hand. Make sure you never leave him unsupervised. If you turn your back for a moment, he may jump off the table.
- Put your puppy into the Stand position, say "Stand," and give him lots of praise and a treat.
- Practice this for just a few minutes every day. Do not expect him to stand for very prolonged periods – he will get bored and resent it.
- Over the course of two to three months, you can train him to stand for longer and longer, so, by the time his adult coat has grown

In time, your Shih Tzu will become relaxed and will enjoy his grooming sessions.

GROOMING TIP

If the table surface is slippery, your dog will feel very insecure, and will not stand properly. A rubber car mat will help to solve the problem.

through, he is thoroughly groomer-friendly.
- Don't forget that "Sit" and "Down" are also useful commands when grooming (see pages 47-48).

TOUCH SENSITIVITY

It is important that your Shih Tzu is comfortable with being touched all over. There is nothing worse than wrestling with a ticklish adult, trying to cut his nails, or checking that he hasn't picked up any grass seeds, when he is phobic about having his feet touched. Prevent any problems by getting your puppy accustomed to head-to-toe handling from a young age.

Feet

- Put your Shih Tzu on your lap and pet him. When he is relaxed, continue to stroke him with one hand, and, with the other hand, gently touch his feet. Stop touching his feet after a couple of seconds and continue to enjoy a cuddle together.
- Repeat the exercise over various sessions, touching his feet for longer periods.
- With further sessions, you should be working towards the time when you can check in between his pads and toes, with the puppy

Teach your puppy to accept having his feet examined.

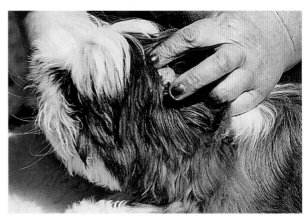

With gentle handling, your puppy will allow you to inspect his ears.

remaining calm – and still – during your examination.

- Always end the sessions with lots of praise, a treat and a game with your puppy's favorite toy.
- When your Shih Tzu needs his nails trimmed, cut off just a little from the tip at a time. You must avoid the quick (the nerves and blood supply) which will bleed profusely if nicked.
- The dewclaws (located above the pad) must also be trimmed regularly (check to see if the puppy has hind dewclaws too). Long dewclaws will curl around and start growing into the skin.

Ears

- Fondle your Shih Tzu's ears – most pups love this, and he will soon be in a dreamy, doggie daze.
- Lift each ear up, and stroke the underside.
- Take a peek inside each ear, then give your Shih Tzu a cuddle and a treat.
- When he is comfortable with his ears being touched, pluck a few hairs out from the opening of the ear to get him used to the procedure when he is older. Ask your vet, groomer or breeder to show you how to do this.

Open Wide

To get your puppy used to having his mouth opened and taking tablets, furnish yourself with a good supply of canine chocolate drops. Do not give him human chocolate, which contains a chemical (theobromine) that is toxic to dogs.

- Put one hand underneath the puppy's lower jaw and one hand over his muzzle, and gently open his mouth.
- Quickly pop in a chocolate drop, then give him lots of praise.
- Your Shih Tzu is likely to be a little grumpy with you – until he suddenly tastes the chocolate.

With a few practices, he will soon look forward to getting his tasty treat, and will be much more willing to cooperate.

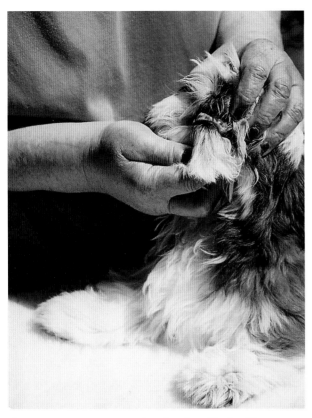

A puppy must get used to having his teeth checked and cleaned.

Dental Care

Small breeds are prone to developing bad teeth, so it is important to get your puppy accustomed to a regular dental care routine.

- Apply a small amount of special canine toothpaste (available from pet stores) on to a small toothbrush.
- Open your puppy's mouth and gently brush the teeth in a downward movement, away from the gums.
- Do not stop if your puppy tries to play with the toothbrush, nor should you get angry – calmly proceed until you are finished, and then reward him.

Teething

When your Shih Tzu is teething (around four months) his gums will become sore as he cuts his adult teeth. He is likely to dribble during this time and chew more than usual, so provide lots of safe, durable chewies.

Regular brushing during the teething period will help to toughen up the gums and relieve some of the pain.

Be warned that your Shih Tzu is likely to be quite snuffly while he is teething, too. This passes once teething is over, but if you are at all concerned, consult your veterinarian.

Eye Care

The Shih Tzu may be a little teary, so daily eye care is required to prevent eye infections and unsightly tear stains.

- Make up a very mild eye-care solution. Use warm water, and perhaps add a small pinch of salt or bicarbonate of soda. A good tear-removing lotion can be used, but use sparingly on a puppy.
- Moisten a cotton pad with some of the solution (make it damp, don't saturate it) and very gently wipe around the eye, removing any debris.
- Use a fresh cotton pad for the other eye to avoid transferring any infection.
- Take your moustache comb (smaller than combs used elsewhere on the body), and very carefully work it through the facial hair. Keep praising your puppy for being well behaved.
- As ever, reward the puppy when you have finished.

Encourage your puppy to go into his crate for a short period during the day.

CRATE TRAINING

As well as putting your Shih Tzu in his crate (page 20) every night, you should also set time aside every day when he is put in the crate for half an hour or so. Put a couple of safe chew toys inside so he can amuse himself, and make sure he has been to the toilet before being put inside (page 36).

Regular crate sessions will prevent the puppy from becoming overly "clingy" as he matures. If he is rarely separated from you, a Shih Tzu does not learn to be independent, and so can become overly distressed if he needs to be left for a short period on his own, or if he is separated from you for a period of time (due to a hospital stay, for example). If he is used to spending time on his own, any separation anxiety behavior (page 58) should be prevented.

SOCIALIZATION

Socialization – a puppy's exposure to life experiences – is the most important part of your Shih Tzu's early education. Many adult dogs have phobias about harmless objects simply because they have never encountered them before. A scared dog is an unpredictable dog, one that could snap at someone or something out of fear. Prevent this by making your puppy bomb-proof against everything life throws at him. Your hard work will provide your puppy with the best possible start in life and will prevent many headaches later on.

The sooner you start, the better. Because you won't be able to take your puppy out in public until he is fully vaccinated, invite friends and family around for a puppy socialization party, and arrange for the puppy to encounter some of the following:

- Someone using a walking stick
- Someone in a wheelchair
- A child in a carriage or stroller
- Someone wearing a personal stereo/ sunglasses/hat/motorcycle helmet
- Someone carrying an umbrella
- Someone riding a bicycle
- Someone on a microscooter/skateboard/ rollerblades
- People of both sexes, of all different ages and ethnic backgrounds
- Someone using a hairdryer and vacuum cleaner
- Someone carrying balloons
- A washing machine doing a fast-spin cycle.

Gradually introduce your puppy to the outside world.

You can also drive your puppy around a busy town center. From the safety of the car, he can be introduced to the big, wide world, with its huge buses, noisy trucks, and car alarms.

Your regular trips will also get the puppy used to car travel. Puppies are sometimes sick on their first few outings, but the more they travel, the better they adapt. Shih Tzus usually love car journeys, as they so enjoy being near their beloved owners.

Once your puppy is vaccinated, you can increase his socialization program.

• Take the puppy in a carrier on a train, bus, or other public transportation.

• Walk your Shih Tzu near ladders, mirrored windows, and construction sites.

• Visit a supermarket parking lot where he will encounter shopping carts and baskets, slow-moving traffic and lots more people.

• Take your puppy in an elevator/on an escalator.

The list is endless! Use your imagination and get your puppy used to as many different situations as you can. Every experience he has in his early weeks will make him a happier more confident dog for the future.

Overcoming Fears

While you are socializing your Shih Tzu, your reactions are crucial. If your puppy encounters something new, he will be a little unsure as to how to react. He will look to you for clues. If you are nervous, fearful that he will be scared, he will pick up on your anxiety, believing that the new object is a threat. If you are laid-back and relaxed, the puppy will realize there is nothing to fear.

If he does take exception to something,

Encourage your puppy to overcome his fears by adopting a reassuring but no-nonsense attitude.

The well-socialized Shih Tzu will take all new experiences in his stride.

reassure him matter-of-factly. Increase his exposure to the item until he is confident. For example, if he takes a dislike to children on skateboards, buy a skateboard and put it in the room in which he spends most of his time.

- When you take your puppy out for his walk, enlist the help of a child to ride the skateboard slowly, at a good distance from the puppy, while you walk past.
- Give the puppy treats intermittently to keep him focused on you, and to reward him for ignoring the skateboard.
- End of lesson – now go and have some fun together.
- For the next session, move the skateboard a fraction closer (don't overdo it – or you might reinforce the phobia).
- Over the course of many sessions, gradually move the skateboard closer, until your Shih Tzu doesn't even blink when he passes it.
- If, at any stage, he shows a fearful reaction, act calmly (don't coddle him), and move the skateboard a little further away, finding a comfortable distance for the puppy before bringing the skateboard closer again.

Puppy Parties

Some dog clubs run puppy socialization classes where young puppies can socialize together. It is important that your puppy learns how to relate to other dogs and how to understand and use canine "language" and behavior to communicate. These classes are great "pre-school" introductions before your Shih Tzu enrolls at a real training class.

OBEDIENCE TRAINING

You can teach an old dog new tricks, but you can usually teach them quicker to a young dog. A Shih Tzu puppy is as bright as a button and is a joy to train. Yes, Shih Tzus can be obstinate and are not as naturally "work-oriented" as the Border Collie, for example, but training will strengthen your relationship and will allow you to share lots of fun along the way. It will result in a well-mannered, obedient dog that you can be proud of.

Puppy Classes

Your veterinary clinic should be able to tell you about training classes in your area. Before enrolling your Shih Tzu puppy, go along and watch one of the sessions. Is it well organized? Is there a calm, friendly atmosphere? What methods are used? If the classes rely on punitive measures rather than positive reward-based methods, you are advised to go elsewhere.

When you attend a class, do not be overprotective of your Shih Tzu – it is very rare for puppies to harm each other. It is best to let all the puppies determine social standing. They will soon make friends, or work out who to avoid, and they aren't shy in telling an overboisterous pup to cool it if he is getting to be a nuisance.

If you behave like a neurotic parent, you will reinforce your Shih Tzu's fears of the dog concerned and make the situation worse.

Of course, if you have real concerns about a particular dog, talk to the class organizer.

Once your Shih Tzu has finished his puppy course, you should carry his training on to a more advanced class. He will benefit from meeting more dogs, and will enjoy having something to tax his brain. You might even want to consider getting involved in a doggie sport, such as Agility or Competitive Obedience (see Chapter Six).

SMART DOGS

Clicker-training is becoming a very popular method of training. It involves a small plastic box which fits comfortably in the hand, and which makes a distinctive "click" when pressed with the thumb. A click is best described as a "yes" marker, something which tells the dog precisely when he has done something that pleases you.

The first stage is to establish that the click is a reward. Every time your Shih Tzu performs a desirable behavior in training, click and reward the puppy by giving a treat. Very soon, the puppy will associate the click with a reward.

Eventually, you will give a click only when the very best behavior is given. For example, when you first start training, you might give a click whenever your Shih Tzu sits. With further training, you should only click when your Shih Tzu sits straight and promptly.

Clickers are available from most pet stores. Why not buy one and try it out? It can be used easily on all the training exercises in this section.

Clicker-training is a rewarding and effective method of teaching.

Healthy Rewards

Successful training relies on your Shih Tzu wanting to cooperate. If he finds the experience enjoyable, he is likely to remain an eager, willing pupil. If he is bored and disinterested, he will learn little.

Keep training sessions short and fun, and use the reward that best motivates your dog. For some dogs it is praise and a cuddle, others work hard for a game with their favorite toy, but the majority prefer food treats. You can find suitable treats from pet stores – buy small treats which can be eaten quickly and choose something which isn't too messy (or you'll end up with gooey fingers and pockets). The most important thing is that the treat should be something which your Shih Tzu absolutely loves – remember, if the dog's "wages" are low, his performance will be too.

Make sure that your Shih Tzu's food allocation is adjusted to take the treats into account, or you will soon end up with a Shih Tzu that is too big to move, let alone train!

Using fresh fruit or vegetables as a reward avoids any weight increase. Some dogs love diced carrot, for example. There are even Shih Tzus that regard peaches, apples, bananas, and peas as treats!

Come

This is the most important exercise a puppy can learn, preventing your Shih Tzu from getting lost, or coming to any harm (e.g., you can call him back if he is running towards a road). Generally, Shih Tzus love being close to their

Make sure you sound exciting so that your puppy really wants to come to you.

owners, and so poor recall (coming when called) is rarely a serious problem – provided training is given from a young age.

This exercise should be started with your new puppy within the first couple of days of bringing him home. Young Shih Tzu puppies love to follow their owners around the house, so exploit this to your advantage before the puppy becomes more independent (around the five- to six-month stage).

- Enlist the help of a friend or family member.
- Ask your assistant to kneel on the floor and to hold the puppy (also on the floor).
- Sit a short distance in front of the puppy and call him to you, saying "Fido, Come!"
- Act in a really exciting way, using a fairly high-pitched voice, animated facial expressions, and clap your hands or hold your arms out wide. You can also offer a treat or the puppy's favorite toy. You want to make yourself irresistible to the puppy.

- As soon as the puppy reaches you, click (if you are clicker-training), give lots of praise, give him a cuddle, and also give a treat or a toy.
- Gradually increase the distance between you and the puppy, acting in the same exciting way every time.
- Make a hide-and-seek game out of your training sessions to keep them fun and to teach your Shih Tzu to track you down if you are out of sight. Hide behind the sofa and call your puppy, hide under a blanket, hide in another room or behind a bush in the yard.
- Only let your Shih Tzu off the lead in a public place when you are certain that his recall is 100 percent reliable. Until that time, keep your dog on an extending lead.
- Never shout at your puppy if he takes a long time to reach you. This will teach him not to come!

Sit

The Sit is another useful exercise, which can stop your Shih Tzu in his tracks whatever he is doing. Remember, puppies can't run out of an open gate if they are sitting, or steal a biscuit from the coffee table, or get themselves into most other forms of mischief.

- Hold a treat in your hand, and show it to your puppy.
- He will follow the treat with his head to get to it.
- Slowly bring your hand just above his head, so that he has to lean back into the Sit position in order to reach it.

Hold a treat above your puppy's head to encourage him to go into the Sit.

- As soon as his bottom touches the floor, click (if you are using a clicker), say "Sit," and give him the treat.
- It will probably take a few practices for your Shih Tzu to understand what is expected of him. He might jump up to get the treat, bark at it, and try every other trick in his repertoire. Just keep trying and he will get there in the end.
- With practice, you can stop luring the dog into position with the treat – he will Sit from your voice command. Always give an occasional treat to keep him interested.
- Incorporate the Sit into your Shih Tzu's everyday life – ask him to sit before you give

him his food bowl, or just before you open the front door. The more your Shih Tzu practices the exercise, the more responsive he will become.

- Once he has mastered the sit in the peace and quiet of your home and yard, introduce a few distractions. Ask someone to walk past while you ask your Shih Tzu to sit. Train in a busy public place. With time, your Shih Tzu should sit whenever you ask him to, regardless of what is going on around him.

INCIDENTAL TRAINING

A good training tip is to say "Sit" or "Down" and praise and reward your Shih Tzu whenever you notice that he sits or lies down during the day. This will help to reinforce, in your dog's mind, the association between the word and the action.

Down

The Down is an extension of the Sit, with the advantage that, once down, your Shih Tzu is more likely to stay in position. It can also be used to settle your dog if you are in a public place or visiting friends.

- Ask your Shih Tzu to sit (see above).
- Show him a treat again, and slowly bring it down so that it is just in front of his paws.
- He is likely to stoop down to reach the treat, but do not let him have it until his tummy touches the floor. Be patient, he will work it out eventually.
- When he does lie down, click (if applicable), say "Down," give him the treat, and give lots of praise.

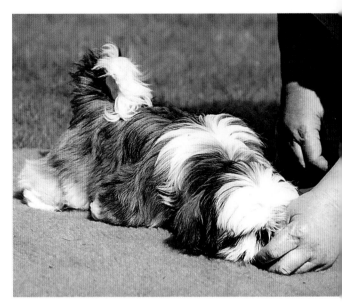

Lower the treat towards the floor, and your puppy will follow his nose and go into the Down.

- Keep practicing until the treat can be withdrawn, and the dog will lie down when instructed.
- Still give an occasional treat – when your Shih Tzu lies down quickly, for instance – to keep him working hard for you.
- As with the Sit, gradually introduce distractions. The ultimate aim is for your Shih Tzu to go down instantly, whatever is going on around him – even if he is running after another dog. Practice little and often, remembering to keep the session fun, and success will be yours.

Stay

The Stay is a little tough to teach, as Shih Tzu puppies are busy little creatures that hate being still. They love being close to their owners, which is a great advantage when teaching your

Work at the Stay in easy stages.

dog lead training or to come when called, but a bit of a disadvantage with this exercise. This can be overcome by showing your Shih Tzu that he will be rewarded with your company if he co-operates.

- Ask your Shih Tzu to go Down (page 48).
- Using your most authoritative voice, tell him "Stay," and put your hand out in front of you, with your palm facing forward.
- Wait a couple of seconds, then click, praise him and give him a treat.
- Next, put your dog in the Down position, take a step back, and ask him to Stay. After just three seconds, step forward to reward him. Give him a cuddle and lavish praise on him so he feels very proud of himself.

- Gradually increase the length and distance of the Stay. Every now and then, stop and play a game with your Shih Tzu as a reward, and to prevent him from becoming bored.
- If, at any point, your Shih Tzu breaks the Stay and comes to you, put him back in position and try again – this time asking him to stay for a shorter length of time and distance.
- Only increase the time and distance very gradually and do not try to do too much too soon.
- If your Shih Tzu looks as if he is about to break his Stay, remind him to "Stay" and give your hand signal again.
- Once your Shih Tzu will reliably Down-Stay for a good length of time and at a reasonable distance, then repeat the exercise – this time starting the dog in the Sit position. Dogs are more likely to break the Sit-Stay (the Down requires more effort to get up), but, having mastered the Down-Stay, your Shih Tzu knows what is expected of him and the Sit-Stay shouldn't pose too many problems.

Collar Comfort

At first, put your Shih Tzu's collar on for just a few minutes every day. Distract him when the collar is on, by giving a treat and playing a game with him. This should prevent him from scratching at the collar. If he is having fun, and the collar is initially put on very loosely, he probably won't even realize it is there.

As he gets used to the collar, it can be tightened a little more every day, until you get to the ideal fit where you can put just two

Give your puppy plenty of encouragement when you start lead training.

Soon he will be happy to walk on the lead, keeping pace with you.

fingers underneath. This is snug enough to prevent your puppy backing out of the collar (something Shih Tzus seem particularly talented at), and sufficiently loose so as not to cause discomfort.

Never leave the puppy unsupervised when he is wearing a collar (particularly a loose one), as it could get caught on something. A collar with a plastic fastening which clips together (pages 21-22) is safer than an unyielding buckle collar, as it gives way under pressure.

Leading The Way

When your puppy is comfortable wearing his collar, attach a very light lead to the collar (a harness is not recommended). Keep the lead so loose that the puppy isn't aware of the lead. If the puppy moves, you should move with him, so that no pressure is exerted. If the puppy feels the lead tighten, he is likely to jump around like a dog possessed, and will be doubly suspicious next time you try to use the lead on him. Walk around the room, encouraging the puppy to follow you – or, ideally, walk next to you – all the time keeping the lead loose.

After a few sessions, try the following.

- Put the puppy in the Sit position, on your left side.
- Hold the lead in your right hand, with the left hand holding the excess slack.
- Take a few steps forward, encouraging the puppy to walk with you.
- Say your puppy's name so that he will look at you while he is walking. This gets him into the good habit of keeping focused on you.
- Praise him when he walks well, click, say "Walk" or "Heel," or whatever command word you want to use. Stop and give him a treat.
- Practice little and often, until he is walking close to, and level with, your left leg (neither lagging forward nor surging ahead).
- If he starts falling behind, say his name in an excited way to speed up, and praise him as soon as he puts more of a spring in his step.
- If he surges ahead, don't get involved in a tug-of-war – just stop. Your Shih Tzu is pulling in order to get to something (usually the park) more quickly. If you stop when he pulls, he quickly learns that pulling is counter-productive.
- When he is walking well beside you in a straight line, start to introduce more variety, at first making gradual curves and slowly making the turns more pronounced.
- Practice also increasing and decreasing your pace, all the time encouraging your Shih Tzu to concentrate on you, and remembering always to give lots of praise when he does well.
- Finish every session with a game so your Shih Tzu can let his hair down and have a good run and play session.

CHAPTER FOUR

THE ADOLESCENT SHIH TZU

The sleepless nights and house-training accidents are now a thing of the past. All your hard work has paid off, and your Shih Tzu has passed his puppyhood with flying colors. Now there's just one more hurdle before you can enjoy a settled life together – adolescence.

Doggie teenagers, like their human counterparts, are in something of a no-man's-land between infancy and maturity. Hormones start kicking in between nine and fifteen months, though sometimes it can start as early as five to six months. Despite the dog's physical development, mentally he is still very much a puppy that has a lot of maturing to do.

It is during this stage that your Shih Tzu may start to test your authority and assert his own independence. Perhaps he will refuse to come when called, or start sleeping on your bed if it is usually out of bounds. There's no need to become a tyrant about it; you just need to be firm and consistent.

If your Shih Tzu gets on the bed, tell him "Off" firmly. If he refuses, repeat the command, and lift him off the bed and place him back on the floor. Even if you are tired, or if it is the tenth time he has leaped on to the bed in one evening, never ignore a transgression of the rules. If you do turn a blind eye, you will be setting a dangerous precedent that your bright little Shih Tzu won't forget in a hurry. Remember, everyone in the family should follow the same rules, or all your work will be in vain.

This chapter deals with some of the problems you may encounter during your Shih Tzu's adolescence. Don't have nightmares – most owners breeze through this period with very few difficulties. If you do experience a problem that you cannot deal with, then seek advice. Contact one of the specialist breed clubs for help, talk to an experienced dog trainer who uses reward-based training, or contact a qualified pet behavior counselor. Your vet should be able to recommend someone who can help you.

*Try to understand
what your Shih Tzu
is going through as
he hits adolescence.*

DOMINANT GUARDING

During adolescence, when a dog is working out his position in the "pack," he may develop guarding behaviors. This may result in guarding his home (see Barking, page 56), or his possessions, such as his bed, toys or food bowl. This certainly isn't a common problem in the breed, but if it does occur, it is important to deal with the behavior promptly before it becomes established.

If a dog starts grumbling when you approach his possessions, it is because he feels he has the right to, i.e., that he is superior to you. Often, this behavior is directed towards children in the family, rather than adults. This is why it is so important that puppy training involves everyone right from the very start (see Chapter Three), as training generally engenders respect in a dog.

Preventing the behavior by taking away the puppy's prized possessions and then rewarding him is the best solution (see page 32), but, if the problem appears post-puppyhood, you will need to teach your Shih Tzu that, much as you love him, he does not call the shots.

Give

The "Give" exercise is a very useful tool for the owner of a dominant dog, and can be used when you want to take the dog's blanket, his food bowl, or another treasured possession.

- Call your Shih Tzu to you, and ask him to do some obedience exercises. Praise and reward him when he obliges. This gets him in a compliant frame of mind, and reinforces your authority over him.
- Take your dog's favorite toy and play with it together. Then call him to you, and tell him to "Give." Very gently pull on the toy, so he knows that you want to take the toy from him.
- If he lets you have it, reward him and give the toy straight back. If he growls, say "No" firmly, and ask him again to "Give."
- If he still refuses to give up the toy, tell him "Down," or any other Obedience command. This will remind him who is boss, and he will find it hard to comply with your wishes while still holding the toy.
- Whatever you do, don't let go of the toy – it may take some patience, but is worth it.

Your Shih Tzu must learn to give up his possessions, such as his food bowl, without complaint.

- Don't forget to give him a tasty treat as a reward when he relinquishes the toy; then give the toy right back to him.
- At the end of the training session, take the toy away until the next time you are playing with your Shih Tzu. He must learn that you have control of his toys, and you decide when he can play with them.

Dominance Reduction

Another way of showing your Shih Tzu that you have a superior hierarchical position in the pack is to behave as a canine pack leader would.
- Eat first
- Walk through doors ahead of your dog
- Do not let the dog charge up and down the stairs in front of you
- Do not allow the dog to sleep or sit on your bed or chair

- Above all else, the pack leader would command respect and should be obeyed unquestioningly, so work hard on your Shih Tzu's training and obedience.

Many people misunderstand dominance reduction, and see it as a huge power struggle with the dog. This isn't really the case. You don't need to be a nasty tyrant; you can still have fun with your dog, share lots of cuddles, and generally enjoy life together, but, ultimately, your Shih Tzu needs to see you as the boss!

Once respect has been established, then you can be more flexible. For example, if you want to watch a late-night film in bed, with your dog on your lap, then let him on to the bed. But it is on condition that, the moment you want him to get off, he will oblige immediately.

If your dog is showing dominance tendencies, do not allow him to decide where he sleeps.

BARKING

Some dogs, particularly males, can see it as their duty to warn their owners whenever someone approaches the house. A guarding instinct is not uncommon in Tibetan and Chinese breeds – the Lhasa Apso, who features in the Shih Tzu's development (see Chapter One) is renowned for it. The courageous Shih Tzu has no real awareness of his own size, and this aptly named Lion Dog won't be silenced if he perceives a threat to his home or his loved ones.

It is quite useful to have a dog that will bark when someone approaches the house. The Shih Tzu doesn't have a bark that befits a small dog, and a stranger wouldn't know from that bark

Stop your dog from barking by asking him to perform a trick, or carry out an Obedience exercise.

that it is just a little Shih Tzu on the other side of the door.

However, the difficulty begins when your brave little dog barks at every unusual sound he hears – and keeps on yapping, even after you have told him to be quiet. Then, you can soon be driven to distraction!

Voicing Concerns

On no account should you attempt to gag your Shih Tzu entirely. It is natural for dogs to bark, and they do so for many reasons. In most cases, a dog barks as a warning sign, but he may also bark because of boredom or frustration. If you just silence your dog without getting to the root cause of why he is barking in the first place, then he will soon find other ways of expressing himself (e.g., destruction or self-mutilation).

Assess the occasions when your Shih Tzu barks. If he sits on a chair all day, looking out of the window, waiting for an excuse to bark, it's likely that he is bored. Take him out for more walks, or for more stimulating walks, play more together, provide him lots of safe toys.

Diversionary Tactics

If you ask your Shih Tzu to sit, or to come to you, he will soon be quiet. It's difficult for a dog to bark while listening to his owner and following obedience commands. Keep a pot of mouthwatering treats with you, wherever you are, to distract your dog when he barks.

Introduce the command "Quiet" and give a reward and lots of praise when he obeys. Some trainers use the command "Speak" when a dog

BARKING UP THE WRONG TREE

Shih Tzus develop very close bonds with their owners, and many become quite "chatty," communicating vocally with their human family.

You may well find that your Shih Tzu likes to say "hello" and to tell you his news when you come into the house. This canine conversation could consist of a whine, a bark, and a grumbling sound (every dog's "tone of voice" is unique), but this should never be confused with barking.

is barking; they can then control the behavior by asking the dog to bark on command and to be "Quiet" on command.

On no account should you start yelling at the dog to be quiet if he barks. This will only agitate him further and encourage him to bark even more – your dog will think you are "barking" at a threat, too.

Provided all family members consistently distract your dog when he is noisy, peace will soon return to your home.

BEGGING

Shih Tzus are renowned for begging. They seem to know that they are seriously cute and that it is hard for people to resist them, and so they make the most of it.

If you followed the advice earlier in this book, you will have discouraged your puppy from begging, and, by adolescence, your Shih Tzu will know that begging gets him nowhere. If those big puppy eyes melted your willpower, though, don't despair, there's still time to turn

your naughty little scrounger into a model family dog.

- Resolve never to give your dog a reward if he begs. If you are eating and he begs, ignore him – however hard it is.
- Being a companion breed, some Shih Tzus will crave attention if they feel they are being neglected – i.e., if they are not the center of attention! As with begging for food, do not reward your demanding dog by giving him your attention, just ignore him. Wait a little while, and when your Shih Tzu has stopped fussing, reward him by having a game or running through a couple of Obedience exercises. Ignoring the dog sounds much easier than it is, of course; many Shih Tzus

The Shih Tzu is highly intelligent and will be quick to find food opportunities.

could win an Oscar for their begging act, but if you give your dog a cuddle or a treat for his performance, you will only encourage him further.

• Remember, the no-begging rule should be enforced by all family, friends, and anyone else who has contact with your dog. One person's failure to uphold the rule will undo all your hard work.

SEPARATION ANXIETY

The Shih Tzu was bred to be a companion dog; it is in his veins, and he is never happier than when in the company of his human family. However, most Shih Tzus are fairly independent and resourceful, and will be quite happy if left on their own for a couple of hours. However, some dogs go berserk, barking to call their owners back, scratching at the door and the carpet, and destroying furniture, and anything else within reach, out of sheer desperation.

This is the behavior of a disturbed and unhappy dog – and there is absolutely no need for it. A dog must learn to be left alone so that he is calm and confident, awaiting your return.

All too often, a puppy goes from the constant companionship of his littermates to becoming the center of attention in his new home. His owner probably arranged to take time off work to settle the puppy in and work on his toilet-training. Eventually, the puppy is left entirely on his own for four hours or more until his owner comes home.

He has been plunged from maximum attention to absolutely no attention, and so becomes upset, bored and frustrated. He barks, rips up the carpet, chews the sofa and scratches at the door, and then, eventually, his owner returns. In the puppy's eyes, his destruction resulted in his owner coming back. So the next time he is left, he repeats the behavior.

What Not To Do

The worst thing you can do if you return home to find a trail of destruction is to shout at your dog. Your Shih Tzu will not be able to understand that you are shouting because he ripped up the carpet an hour – or even five minutes – ago. Instead, he will think you are shouting because he has just greeted you. Then, your Shih Tzu will start to dread your return, thinking you will shout again. This will make him even more anxious when he is left alone, and so he may express his distress by becoming more destructive or through soiling. And so the vicious circle continues.

Positive Action

So what should you do? Firstly, bite your tongue. Making your Shih Tzu feel lousy will not mend your sofa, or bring back Aunty Maud's antique vase. Nor will it prevent your dog from wreaking future destruction. Next, review your Shih Tzu's care. Is he being destructive out of boredom?

If you have established that your Shih Tzu is simply craving your attention because he has become overdependent, then you will have to wean him off you, teaching him to be a little more self-reliant.

A crate (pages 20, 42) is an invaluable tool for teaching your Shih Tzu to be more independent. Used properly during a dog's puppyhood, it prevents many problems that are linked with overattachment. If you avoided crate training during your pup's early months, then you will have to start now.

Being able to leave your Shih Tzu for short periods in his crate means you can rest assured not only that your house isn't being wrecked, but also that your dog is safe. However, don't be tempted to ignore the training, and just use the crate when you have to leave your dog on his own. This is very cruel, and will just exacerbate his distress. He must be trained to view the crate as a safe, enjoyable place to be.

- Make the crate as inviting as you can. Line it with some comfortable bedding, put in some interactive toys (such as rubber toys, balls or cubes in which treats are placed), and hide some smelly liver treats around the crate (e.g., under the bedding).
- Sit by the crate with your Shih Tzu, and play with one of his favorite toys.
- Your curious Shih Tzu will probably wander into the crate to nose around. If he doesn't, after a couple of minutes, put the toy in the crate, to encourage him to follow it. Keep the door wide open, so your dog doesn't feel trapped.
- Repeat this "game" many times over the course of several days until your Shih Tzu feels secure in the crate. It is likely, that, when he discovers the food and toys in the crate, he will settle inside to chew on the tasty treats.

Work at leaving your Shih Tzu in his crate for short periods.

- Only when your dog is absolutely comfortable being in the crate should you close the door.
- Stay right by the crate, and keep the door closed for just five seconds, before opening it again. It is unlikely that your dog will even notice that the door was closed – he should be too busy with all the fun toys and treats you have provided inside.
- Over a period of several weeks, you should gradually lengthen the time during which the door is shut. Stay in the same room, so your Shih Tzu doesn't feel he is being deserted.
- If your Shih Tzu barks or acts in an otherwise distressed way, do not respond – or you will be rewarding your dog's behavior, and therefore encouraging it.
- Instead, wait for him to be quiet (perhaps even startling him into being quiet by

pretending to sneeze or by dropping some keys on the floor).

- As soon as your dog is quiet, let him out, and make sure that, next time, the treats inside the crate are tastier and the length of time he is kept in is shorter.

- Proceed very gradually, or you will have to start back at square one.

- Once your dog will remain contentedly in the crate for ten minutes, then gradually increase the distance between you and the crate. For example, instead of sitting right next to the crate, sit a couple of feet away. Then further away. Again, proceed very slowly.

- If your dog shows distress when you are five feet away, go back to sitting next to the crate, before gradually increasing your distance.

- With time, you should be able to step outside the room for a few seconds, and then for longer and longer.

- Next, you should remove the negative associations of your exit cues. For instance, put on your shoes and coat, pick up your keys, and then put them back again.

- Then, progress to opening the front door, closing it, and returning to the room he is in. Then stay outside for 10 seconds, then one minute, before returning to him. Gradually extend the length of time for which he is left.

- Repeating his crate training exercises regularly should mean your Shih Tzu will be happy to spend time alone for longer and longer periods. Repeat the exercises even when your dog is "cured" to prevent any separation anxiety from recurring.

- Do remember: a crate is not a substitute dog-sitter, and the dog should never be placed in a crate for unreasonably long periods of time.

DOGGIE DEN

If your Shih Tzu doesn't like his crate, put a blanket over it, so that three of the four sides of the "den" are covered. Some dogs prefer the privacy and coziness this provides.

GROOMED FOR SUCCESS

If you own a Shih Tzu, then, chances are, you will spend a lot of your time grooming him. This is one of the pleasures of owning a long-haired breed. Some owners of pet dogs opt to have the dog's coat clipped to a short, manageable length. But, in some cases, it is the dog's refusal to be groomed that means there is no option other than having the coat clipped short by a professional groomer.

A clipped coat on a pet dog is fine if you are happy with the "puppy" look, but if it was the magnificent coat that first attracted you to the breed, and you would prefer a long-coated dog, then there is no reason why you should compromise, just because your Shih Tzu refuses to be groomed.

Preventing Tantrums

As with all inappropriate behavior, prevention is better than cure. Getting your puppy used to being handled and brushed from a young age should prevent temper tantrums later in life. The trouble is that, because the puppy coat is short and easy to keep tangle-free, many people

TIME ALONE

Remember, no dog should be left for more than four hours at a time. Dogs are pack animals, and it is unfair to expect them to endure long periods devoid of human contact. This is especially the case with a breed like the Shih Tzu, that is very much a "people" dog.

If your Shih Tzu is displaying symptoms of separation anxiety because he is being left for hours on end, it should come as no surprise, and you will need to review how you care for him. It is completely unacceptable to expect a dog to endure being left alone for so long. If necessary, arrange for a dog-friendly neighbor or professional dog-walker to visit your Shih Tzu during the day. Make sure he is played with, petted, and exercised for at least three-quarters of an hour every four hours, so that he receives the human company he so desperately needs.

Remember that the Shih Tzu is very much a people dog, and should never be left alone for long.

do not accustom the dog to being handled all over. Then, when you attempt a full grooming session for the first time during the adolescent months when the coat grows to full length, it is understandable that the dog will object. And if you stop grooming him because he struggles, barks or snaps, his coat becomes more neglected, and the dog learns that aggressive behavior is successful at stopping an unwanted grooming session.

Successful Grooming

If the problems are already established, don't despair – there's no need to resort to having your dog clipped down if you want a long coat. You just need to start from scratch, build up your dog's trust, and progress very slowly (see page 68 for pet trims).

Prevention is better than cure, so get your Shih Tzu used to grooming from the time he arrives home.

- Settle on the sofa, with your Shih Tzu on your lap, and enjoy a cuddle together.
- After a couple of minutes, with your Shih Tzu at his most relaxed, gently stroke him along his spine with the back of his dog brush. Keep talking to him while you do this. He probably won't even notice that you have stopped using your hand to stroke him.
- Every now and then, give him a treat as a reward for accepting contact with the brush. End of session one.
- Repeat several times, and then start stroking your Tzu with the back of the brush over more of his body, such as his chest and legs.
- Don't forget to pet, reassure and give treats, so that your dog views these sessions as truly heavenly experiences.
- If, at any time, your Shih Tzu seems uncomfortable with the brush, stop, and stroke him with your hand. Don't get mad, or your Shih Tzu will associate the brush with your anger, and you will be reinforcing his fears. Slowly introduce the brush again once he is comfortable, and make sure he views it as being an enjoyable experience – e.g., give him some of his favorite treats, and tickle his chest.
- Once he is happy being touched with the back of the brush, lie him on his side and gently lift his front legs so you can move the brush over his tummy. Give extra praise for this, as it is an especially sensitive area.
- Only when you can move the back of the brush all over his body should you move on to very gently stroking your Shih Tzu with

If your youngster objects to being groomed, go back to basics, and restart his training.

the bristled side of the brush. Don't attempt to remove any knots, at first. Just hold a section of coat with one hand and very carefully work the brush through it. (If you hold the hair, it stops you pulling on it while brushing, and your dog will hardly feel that he is being groomed.)

- Do this for just a minute, then give a special treat, lots of praise, and take your Shih Tzu out to the yard for one of his favorite games.
- Over many of these sessions, gradually lengthen the grooming time, always giving a special reward at the end. If your Shih Tzu starts to object, it means you are progressing too quickly for his liking, so shorten the grooming time until he is ready for longer sessions.

NEUTERING

Neutering is often used by pet owners, when a puppy is very young, to forestall the development of problem behavior, but usually poor socialization or training is actually responsible. Neutering is only useful if there is a hormonal cause for the dog's mischief – for example, if the dog is mounting furniture out of sexual frustration, or is aggressive with other dogs due to excess testosterone. Your veterinarian will be able to assess your dog's case and tell you if neutering is likely to be successful.

Even if you have an adolescent angel, you may still want to consider having your Shih Tzu neutered (provided you do not have plans for breeding or showing), as there are many health benefits for your dog. A female is spayed, meaning the womb is removed. This prevents her from developing pyometra, a life-threatening condition which can occur in later life, where the womb fills with pus. Your spayed female will also have a dramatically reduced chance of developing mammary tumors.

Health aside, the convenience of having a spayed female cannot be underestimated. It means you won't have to deal with her seasons, when, every six to nine months, for a period of several weeks, she will become utterly irresistible to every male dog in the county. You will be surprised at how headstrong and sneaky your Shih Tzu can be if she wants to be mated, and many people end up with a pregnant female, despite their vigilance. If this happens, then you will have all the veterinary and whelping costs to pay for, not to mention the difficult task of finding responsible, loving homes for a litter of mixed breeds.

A male dog also benefits from being neutered. Castration, where the testicles are removed, means a reduction in prostate disorders and there is no danger of testicular tumors.

Discuss the pros and cons of neutering with your vet.

Provided it is done early enough, castration can also prevent your dog from developing unsociable behavior such as scent marking, mounting, being aggressive to other dogs plus going AWOL every time a female comes into season in the neighborhood.

There are some disadvantages to neutering. Weight gain is frequently quoted as being an effect of neutering, but this is not the case. It is simply that a neutered dog is usually less active (due to less roaming), and so requires fewer calories. If you do not adjust your dog's food intake, he will put on weight. In some cases, incontinence in spayed bitches can result, but this is rare. In both sexes, the coat can become more luxurious and thick after neutering, though the texture will not change.

As with any surgery, neutering is not without its risks, but the procedure is performed so often that it is considered a routine operation. It is up to you to weigh up the pros and cons, to discuss the issues with your veterinarian, and to make your own decision.

CHAPTER FIVE

THE ADULT SHIH TZU

Considering the Shih Tzu's history as a companion dog, it comes as little surprise that the breed thrives in a family environment. Although the Shih Tzu is not usually suitable for a home with pre-school-age children (page 29), he will flourish around well-behaved older children, provided he is treated with kindness and respect.

Although Shih Tzus can look prim, proper, and haughty, among those they know and love, they are fun-loving and comical, and love to play with their family, whatever their age.

A home with lots of people in it means lots more laps and lots more cuddles – pure Shih Tzu heaven!

EXERCISE

The Shih Tzu may look dainty and fragile, but he should not be coddled. Most Shih Tzus enjoy a good walk, whatever the weather – in fact, some seem to prefer wet weather and delight in rolling in mud to get their coat as filthy as possible!

A fully-grown adult needs a minimum of two 20-minute walks a day. Try to make your walks interesting – in safe areas throw toys for your dog to chase, or hide from your Shih Tzu and encourage him to find you.

Introduce some variety. Instead of performing the same mundane circuit of the local park every day, try new routes, such as through woods or on the beach, or go to different parks. Your Shih Tzu will revel in all the different sights and smells.

Include some lead-walking on hard surfaces a couple of times a week. It will give you an opportunity to practice your dog's lead-training, and also helps to wear down his nails, keeping them in trim.

Wherever you walk, it is a good idea to toilet your dog in your yard before leaving. Never leave home without taking a bag or pooper-scoopers with you so you can always pick up after your dog if he is caught short.

FAMILY FUN

Try to involve your Shih Tzu in your everyday activities. If you need to buy your newspaper from the local shop, take your Shih Tzu out with you for the five-minute walk. Need to visit Aunty for an hour? Why not ask if your Shih Tzu can come along too? The Shih Tzu adores sharing his life with his loved ones, and these activities will help to break up his day.

COMPANION DOGS

Once your Shih Tzu is an adult, you may consider getting a second dog to keep him company. Shih Tzus really enjoy the company of other dogs – particularly their own breed, and will amuse themselves for hours playing with tug-toys, chasing each other or simply sitting together and watching the world go by outside the window. (See page 33 on introducing a new puppy to an adult dog.)

Never consider getting two puppies at the same time – it is much too much hard work, and you will not be able to devote sufficient time to training and socializing each one. Double the Shih Tzu and you double the trouble!

FEEDING

Most owners feed their adult Shih Tzus in the morning and the evening. Make sure you stick to a routine where your dog is fed at the same time every day.

A discussion of the different types of food is on page 24. Do not change your dog's food unless you really have to, in which case a switch to a new brand of food should be done gradually (page 25). Remember also not to pander to your dog, or you will end up with an infuriatingly fussy eater (page 26).

OBESITY

For a breed that is renowned for being picky about its food, there is a surprising number of overweight Shih Tzus. Pampering the dog with table scraps and fatty treats, and feeding whenever the dog demands it (rather than keeping to a strict routine), quickly results in a pudgy dog.

Prevention is essential or serious health problems will result. Weigh out your dog's daily food allocation and do not exceed it. Do not allow him to beg, and make sure friends and family do not feed the dog without asking your permission first (so you can adjust his food accordingly).

Try to feed your Shih Tzu at roughly the same times every day.

COZY WITH POSY

Born into a family of Shih Tzu enthusiasts, Ann Pickburn from Kirk Hammerton, North Yorkshire, England, has never known a life without dogs. So it was natural that her own daughter, Helen, would also grow up surrounded by Shih Tzus.

"My parents showed and judged Shih Tzus, and my father was secretary of the breed club," explains Ann. "I inherited their love of the breed, and Helen (now 12) grew up in a house full of dogs too.

"The dogs took to Helen the moment she was born; one would sleep under her carriage, guarding and protecting her. I know some breeders won't let their puppies go to homes with young children, but I think it depends on the family. If one of my dogs has puppies, I like to be sure that prospective families play by my rules. For children, my rules are: no poking, no prodding, and no disturbing the puppy if he is resting.

"During Helen's life, not one of my dogs has ever snapped at her. They are taught to respect each other. The dogs have rules too. They are not allowed to sleep upstairs, and they are kept away if Helen has friends to visit unless I am sure that the children are used to dogs. Seeing four dogs rush in excitedly can be scary if you are not used to dogs – and some children are brought up in anti-dog homes where they are taught to fear dogs. Another rule is that the dogs are not allowed to pull on the lead if Helen walks them – they are taught to respect Helen as they would respect me.

TOLERANCE

"When children grow up around dogs, they are taught respect and tolerance for another living thing. They also develop a close friendship. Many times, I've heard Helen chatting away to one of the dogs, since she was a young girl.

Helen has developed a special relationship with the family Shih Tzus.

"Helen is closest to her own dog, Posy, who she has had since she was five. They immediately became friends, and now you never see one without the other.

"Dog ownership teaches children about the responsibility of having a pet. Helen bathes Posy, and will feed and exercise the dogs with me.

FAMILY PET

"I think Shih Tzus are ideal family pets. They have a sound temperament, are healthy and live a long time. In some breeds, dogs die at a very young age, but the Shih Tzu usually lives well into his teens.

"When I breed a litter of puppies, there are always tears when the puppies leave, and, of course, when a dog dies. It is hard for a child at the time, but they do learn how to accept loss and cope with it as a fact of life.

"I'm not sure that Helen will follow in my footsteps, and those of her grandparents, and show and judge dogs when she is older. Even if she doesn't show Shih Tzus, I know she will never live without one in her home. It's all she's ever known."

If the dog becomes used to an over-indulgent lifestyle, he will consider it the norm. If you cut down on his food and impose a strict eating regime, your Shih Tzu will try every trick in the book to persuade you to break his diet. Be strong and do not give in to his heart-melting expressions and pitiful whines – it is all for his own good.

What is overweight?

Your Shih Tzu's ideal weight will depend on his height (your veterinarian can give you a precise weight based on your dog's measurements). When you live with a dog, it is very difficult to notice gradual weight increases, so weigh your Shih Tzu every month to monitor any changes. Stand on the scales and make a note of your own weight, and then weigh yourself again while holding your dog. Subtract the first figure from the second to come up with your dog's result.

As a general guide, you should be able to feel your dog's ribs, but they shouldn't be too prominent. Look at your dog's body from above – there should be a definite shape to the body, and you should be able to notice a waistline. If your Tzu's body resembles a house brick, it's time for action!

If your dog is overweight, you should contact your veterinarian. Many practices run weight-loss clinics, and will be able to plan a feeding program for your Shih Tzu. Several food manufacturers have diet/lite versions of their food, so, provided you are strict and do not give in to your Shih Tzu's pleading, shifting the pounds should be relatively simple.

POOR HEALTH

Do not underestimate the effects of obesity. It isn't just an aesthetic consideration; it has many serious health implications. The heart has to work harder and excess pressure is put on the dog's skeleton and joints. The dog is then likely to become less active, making him prone to further weight increase.

GROOMING

Most owners are attracted to the Shih Tzu because of his magnificent coat and they pledge to keep their dogs in long coats. However, the majority of pet owners renege on their promises. When you consider the length of time it takes to keep the coat in order (at least 20 minutes every day and about two hours for bathing and grooming once a week), it comes as little surprise that most pet owners opt to have the coat trimmed. Do not feel guilty about having your Shih Tzu sport a shorter coat. It is much better for the dog to be mat-free and comfortable.

Puppy Trim

There's no need to have the coat clipped off entirely. Experienced groomers can do some lovely puppy trims, where the coat is scissored in such a way as to make the dog well into his dotage look as young and as cute as a puppy.

A puppy trim keeps the dog cooler in hot weather, and, most importantly, the coat is easier to maintain. However, you will still need to groom the coat every day to prevent painful tangles and mats.

The puppy trim can look very attractive, and it certainly cuts down on the workload.

Bathing

On average, a long-coated Shih Tzu needs a bath every week. A clipped/trimmed dog will not need bathing as frequently – maybe once every three to four weeks. At least once a week, male dogs will need a good tummy wash to remove any urine dribbles, and both sexes need their bottoms washed to remove any build-up of fecal matter.

- Be prepared. Make sure you have a rubber mat in the bath or shower cubicle to prevent your dog slipping and feeling insecure, and have your shampoo, conditioner, comb, and towel all at hand.
- Place the dog on the mat, say "Stand" (page 39), and talk to him all the time to reassure him.
- Using a shower attachment, gently wet his body with warm water. Wet in the direction from the tail to the head. (The dog is most sensitive about his head and face, so you want it to be wet for as little time as possible.

- Use a mild dog shampoo – one that will not strip the natural oils from the coat. Place a small amount in a bowl and dilute it with some water. Then work the shampoo into the dog's coat.

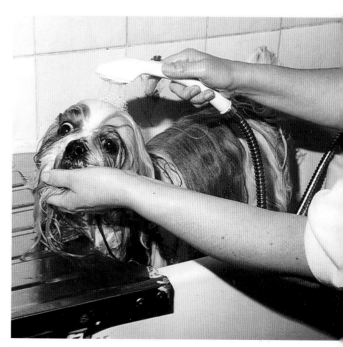

Test the water to make sure it is lukewarm, and then wet the coat thoroughly.

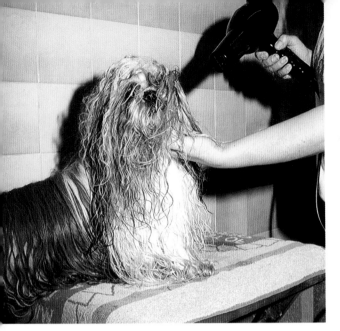

Check the setting before using a hair dryer.

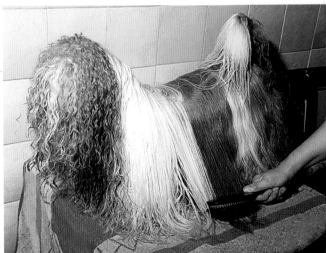

The coat is brushed through as it dries.

- Make sure you get right down to the skin. Again, start at the tail and work your way up to the head.
- Rinse the shampoo away thoroughly, this time starting at the head (so that the head has shampoo on it for just a short amount of time). Shield the eyes so that no shampoo gets into the eyes.
- Apply some canine conditioner to your hands and then smooth it into the coat.
- Using a metal comb, brush the conditioner through the coat, and then rinse thoroughly (starting at the head and working towards the tail).
- When you are certain that there is no shampoo or conditioner residue left in the coat, stop rinsing.
- Praise the dog, give him a treat, and wrap him in a towel. Make sure the head is dried first, so your Shih Tzu feels comfortable.
- Pat away all the excess moisture from the coat and carry him to your grooming area.

Drying

- Continue to towel-dry the coat. Place sections of the coat in a towel and squeeze the moisture out. Do not rub. This is especially important if your Shih Tzu is long-coated.
- The coat now needs drying. You can use a normal hair dryer, but it is probably worth investing in a professional canine dryer with a stand.
- This will free up one of your hands so you can hold the dog with one hand, and brush him with another (a difficult task if you also have to hold a hair dryer).
- The dryer should be on a medium setting – keep checking the temperature to make sure it does not get too hot.
- Also make sure that the dryer isn't too close to the dog or his skin could get burned.
- Dry the coat in sections, all the time brushing the coat to keep it tangle-free and straight.
- At the end, don't forget to give your Shih Tzu a treat and a cuddle as a reward.

REGULAR CHECKS

TEETH

The teeth should be cleaned at least once a week (see page 41). It is also worth feeding tartar-control treats occasionally (available from pet stores) which help to keep the teeth clean.

NAILS

These should also be checked once a week. Healthy adult dogs that are receiving an adequate amount of exercise rarely need their nails trimmed. Puppies, older dogs, and those that do not get enough road-walking may require a trim.

If the nails are overly long, the ends should be trimmed carefully using a pair of guillotine-type nail clippers. Never cut into the quick, as this will be very painful to your dog and can cause infection.

It is advisable to ask your veterinarian or groomer to show you what to do.

PADS

Check your dog's pads every day for any foreign bodies, such as thorns or grass seeds. Also check between the toes. If the feet are muddy, rinse them, or the mud can dry in clumps and rub the toes sore. Hair can grow between the pads, causing discomfort. Keep a regular check, and trim if necessary.

EARS

The ears also pick up grass seeds and other clutter on your dog's walks. Check them every day when you give your Shih Tzu his daily brush.

Also look inside the ears. At the first sign of any change in their smell or color, or if your Shih Tzu keeps shaking his head or pawing at his ear, see your veterinarian, who will be able to treat the infection or mites.

Long strands of hair grow at the top of the ear canal, and these will need to be removed by plucking. This is a skilled job, so ask a professional groomer to show you how.

EYES

Every day, the eyes will need to be bathed (see page 41).

If tartar accumulates on the teeth, they will need to be cleaned with a tooth scaler.

If your Shih Tzu does not wear down his nails naturally, you will need to use a guillotine naill clipper.

Hair grows between the pads, and this may need to be trimmed.

If the ears need cleaning, make sure you do not probe too deeply into the ear canal.

Expert help will be needed to remove the hair that grows inside the ear.

GROOMING YOUR SHIH TZU

All groomers have their own methods, and so it is a matter of working out a routine that suits you and your Shih Tzu.

1. Some groomers have the dog lying on their lap when they work through the undercarriage. First, a comb is used.

2. The undercarriage is brushed through so it is completely tangle-free.

3. The dog is now moved to the table to work on the rest of the coat. The comb is being used to go through the coat in sections.

4. The body coat is then brushed through in sections.

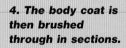

GROOMING YOUR SHIH TZU

5 & 6. The Shih Tzu's coat falls in a parting, and this is created along the line of the back.

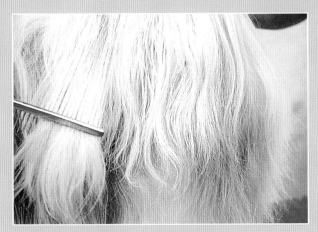 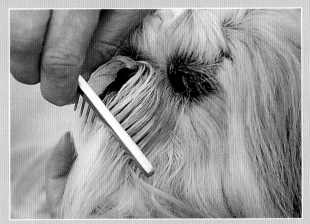

7. The tail needs special attention.

8. The moustache is combed through.

9. The ear is lifted to get to the head furnishings.

TYING A TOPKNOT

1. There are different types of topknot. In the show ring, the hair is usually tied in a single knot. First, the hair is combed upwards.

2. It is secured in place with a hair band.

3. A classic topknot.

The final result: A beautifully groomed Shih Tzu, showing the glamorous coat to its best advantage.

RESCUED DOGS

Every year, hundreds of Shih Tzus end up in rescue organizations in the United Kingdom and the United States. The main reason is the owner's ignorance of the hard work and hours of grooming that are needed to care for a long-coated breed. Many Shih Tzus turn up in shelters with severe mats, that are often so bad they require the dog to be anaesthetised for them to be removed.

Bad breeding is the second reason for abandoned Shih Tzus. Puppy farms (mills) have exploited the public demand for this popular breed by turning out lots of poorly-socialized, badly-bred puppies from parents that were never good examples of the breed in the first place. The result is that many pups with bad temperaments are sold to people who perhaps should not even have a dog (puppy farmers and bad breeders are not scrupulous about who they sell to). These dogs may be snappy and aggressive, soon ending up in rescue and giving the breed a very bad name.

Pauline Read from Abbots Langley, Hertfordshire, England, runs Home Counties Shih Tzu Rescue. In her ten years' experience of breed rescue work, she has seen a number of horror stories, where dogs have arrived at her doorstep severely matted and flea-ridden, with terrible skin conditions.

"People don't seem to realize that Shih Tzus are big dogs in little bodies," she says. "Shih Tzus can be dominant, strong-minded and stubborn. In the wrong home, where the owner spoils them and treats them like babies, the dog will become even more dominant."

BEFORE AND AFTER

Before: Muffin arrived for rehoming in a terrible state. Her coat was completely matted, and she was flea-ridden. Her left eye was closed up. The vet was called in to administer a light anesthetic so that she could be given a thorough examination. Her coat was clipped, and once the hair was removed, an eye infection was diagnosed. She had huge mats on her pads, and when these were removed, it was found she had an infection in her foot caused by a grass seed. Muffin was treated with flea spray, and homoeopathic remedies were used to help her skin.

After: Muffin was rehomed, and within two weeks she was a completely different dog. Her infections had completely cleared up, her skin was improving and her coat was beginning to regrow. Second time lucky, Muffin is now ready to enjoy a happy, healthy life with her new owners.

SHELTER SHIH TZUS

For Paul Post, from Apple Valley, California, his two rescue Shih Tzus are more than simply pets and companions, they are lifesavers.

"Shih Tzus are very lovable dogs, and, as long as I'm alive, we will always have one in our household. I wouldn't live without one!" says Paul.

"We've had rescued dogs before, and gave a home in 1994 to our first Shih Tzu, Woody, who was nine months old at the time. Woody has now been joined by Dok, Shih Tzu number two.

"I prefer rescue dogs; I leave the puppies up to the breeders. There are too many dogs that need good homes. Most people forget that when you bring home a little fluffball Shih Tzu puppy, it won't stay like that forever. When the puppy grows up, some people lose interest and then the dog is sent off to a shelter.

"In his last home, Woody was left outside 24 hours a day. He ran the streets and tried to fight larger dogs that he came into contact with (whether they were fenced-up or not). He was also a cat-chaser, and wasn't housebroken. We jumped at the chance of having him. Woody was just nine months old when he came to our home and it took just a couple of days for me to train him to notify a family member when he needed to go outside.

"Dok was a little different. He had been constantly tied up to a tree, in the dirt, all day long. I believe he was brought in at night, but he wasn't housebroken. He was also nine months old when he came to our home.

"There are disadvantages to taking on a rescued Shih Tzu, many of whom have a bad history of abuse. Sometimes, the dog has adopted bad habits or has jaded opinions of the world. Woody still has a few bad habits that just cannot be broken. He has to be watched very closely around young children. Dok's bad habit is his love of being the center of attention, which is the standard trait of a Shih Tzu. He's one lovable furball.

Woody (left) and Dok: These two little dogs have completely transformed their owner's life.

"Training and grooming are the two chief considerations for people thinking of adopting a rescued Shih Tzu. Time should be taken to train the Shih Tzu – and they are much smarter than most people realize. It's important that they're shown who is the boss. A lot of people tend to baby their Shih Tzus instead of training them. They can be very stubborn dogs, and it is important that they know, early on, that the handler is the alpha dog. Otherwise, they'll walk all over you.

"The bad habits won't be solved overnight, a week or even a month later. It will take quite a while for the Shih Tzu to recover, but with time, affection and patience, the majority will get there in the end.

"As well as being able to help Woody and Dok, they have helped me a great deal, too. When Woody came to live with us, I was on chemotherapy for Non-Hodgkin's Lymphoma, a condition which can kill within months if not treated in the right way. We attended every Obedience class that I could go to. That got me out of the house one hour a day, three days a week. My doctors at the hospital couldn't believe how quickly I recuperated. My progress was that of someone who had been on chemo for a year, although I had only been on it for three months.

"I really had no idea what my goal was for

Woody's training. I was just socializing him at the Obedience classes, which helped with the bad habits. Then, a friend suggested I show Woody at the Palm Springs Kennel Club show. I had never entered an Obedience competition before, yet we showed in Novice A against 18 dogs and we walked away with second place. That was a big accomplishment for the both of us, and we were hooked from that day on. To this date, Woody and I show at least once a month. When Dok came on the scene, we allowed the dogs to get familiar with each other, and then started Dok's training too.

WHAT'S UP, DOK?

"In October 1997, one week before another dog show, I had a heart attack. Dok helped me to get out of the hospital bed much quicker than my doctor advised, and the hospital was adamant that I should not attend the dog show. However, I was released from the hospital on Thursday, and on Sunday we were at the dog show, where Dok took fifth place out of 35 dogs.

Paul Post with Dok, celebrating one of his many triumphs.

Putting Dok through his paces.

TOUCH WOOD

"Then, in February of 1998, I had a tube placed in my heart artery, and was put on blood thinners. Three weeks later, when I attempted to take Woody out of my truck, his head hit my lower jaw, which really swelled up. Within a few days, I was back in the doctor's office, thinking the blood thinners were responsible for making my jaw swell. However, it turned out to be a tumor that I was unaware I had. Woody saved my life.

"I was in remission for four years, until that incident. For the next year, we trained together one hour a day, three times a week. I stuck to that schedule as much as possible between chemo and radiation treatments, and still insisted on competing at dog shows once a month.

"In November 1998, another tumor showed up – in my abdomen, this time. I was given a bone marrow transplant and the next four months were filled with chemo treatments in the hospital. Unfortunately, I was unable to show Woody and Dok during those four months but we did train as much as possible. I left the hospital on March 15, 1999, and showed Woody in Utility just three weeks later. As before, the doctors were amazed at how fast I recuperated. I couldn't have done it without the help of my wife, our son Jeff, and, of course, Woody and Dok."

Fortunately, the Shih Tzu is a long-lived breed.

"The Shih Tzu is a dog, not a fluffy, cuddly toy. I've even had people approach me for a Shih Tzu as a present for their baby to play with!

"Perhaps at 10 months to a year, or after the female's first season, hormones start kicking in, the Shih Tzu becomes more dominant, and the coat changes. If you do not keep on top of the emerging adult coat, it will mat very quickly.

"Many of the dogs that come to me have passed through three or four homes. Someone passes the dog on to a friend, or someone down their street, who then can't cope... and so the dog is passed on to someone else again. Eventually, the animal will end up in rescue.

"Luckily, the Shih Tzu is very resilient, and loves people, so, with lots of love and care, the majority are transformed into adorable, trusting little souls, who can be rehomed – to the right family."

If you would like to find out more about adopting a rescued dog, contact your national kennel club for details of approved Shih Tzu rescue organizations.

VETERAN CARE

The Shih Tzu is a long-lived breed that remains young at heart whatever his age. Technically, a dog is considered a veteran at the age of seven, when most Shih Tzus are still as active and mischievous as puppies.

However, at this age, it is worth considering switching your dog's food to a senior variety that is specifically made for maintaining the immune systems of older dogs. "Senior" foods often contain less protein, as less energy is required. Excess protein in the diet can be a contributing factor in kidney disease, a fairly common problem in older dogs.

Every dog matures differently, of course, but generally an older dog will sleep more, and

The veteran Shih Tzu will probably feel more comfortable if he is kept in a puppy trim.

exercise and eat less. The coat may become thinner and less lustrous, and dark-colored dogs will gray a little around the muzzle.

During your dog's daily grooming, be extra-vigilant for any changes – such as lumps or bumps – and consult your veterinarian if you notice anything. Early disease detection gives your Shih Tzu the best chance of being successfully treated.

Because older dogs are more prone to illness, you should get your veteran checked over by a veterinarian every six months, even if you consider he is in good health.

Diet

Some oldies lose their appetite. Health problems may be responsible, such as kidney disease, so a loss of appetite should always be investigated by the veterinarian. Here are some tips for encouraging your oldie to eat.

- Very old dogs can be pampered. If your Shih Tzu is really off his food, try every trick in the book and ignore the previous rules (page 26) about not giving in to your dog's whims!
- If your dog is fed a dry complete food, try wet food, which many dogs love. There are several brands (in small foil cartons) made specifically for small breeds, that look good enough for humans to eat!
- Tempt his appetite by putting some fresh flaked fish (minus the bones) into his ordinary food. Chicken meat is another favorite.
- Warm his food slightly to release the aroma.
- Cat food (senior food) is another short-term option.
- Switch to three or four small meals a day so your Shih Tzu can eat little and often.

Exercise

Again, throw out the rule book. Do not force your oldie to walk two 20-minute walks a day. If he is looking tired after 10 minutes, carry him home. Go with the flow, and adapt your care and routines according to your dog's needs.

Remember that it is important still to keep your dog's brain ticking over, so continue to play games together, and do not let him become bored by life. Change your walks every now and again, give him a new toy to play with, or teach him a new Obedience exercise or trick. All these things will help to blow away the cobwebs.

SAYING GOODBYE

It's one of life's sad facts: that dogs do not live as long as humans, and there will come a time when you will have to say goodbye to your Shih Tzu. Most of us hope that our dogs will die peacefully in their sleep and that we will not have to "play God;" sadly, few dogs die this way, and so the question of euthanasia has to be addressed.

Euthanasia is a painless way of ending an animal's suffering via an injection of barbiturates. It is a peaceful way for the animal to die, similar to the dog falling into a deep sleep. Most veterinarians can arrange home visits to perform euthanasia, which many owners – and animals – find less stressful than going to the veterinarian's office.

The Right Decision

Whatever happens, you should never consider prolonging your Shih Tzu's suffering because of your own feelings.

It is natural to want your dog to live as long as possible, because you love him so much, but consider your Shih Tzu's quality of life. It is selfish to keep him alive, if it is not in the dog's best interests. Your Shih Tzu is your responsibility. If he is in pain, and there is nothing more that can be done for him, then you must discuss with your veteterinarian the possibility of euthanasia.

Making Plans

It is advisable to consider how you would like the body to be disposed of while your Shih Tzu is still young and healthy. No one is in a fit state to make a decision at the time an animal is put to sleep – with all the upset, it is very easy to do something that you later regret.

Some people like to bury their pets on their own property (local regulations permitting), others arrange for cremation and ask that the ashes are returned to them. There are many private pet crematoria (ask your veterinarian or search on the Internet for suitable companies), or your veterinarian can also arrange for a cremation.

Coping With Grief

Losing a pet is a devastating experience, and it is perfectly natural to grieve. A dog is a member of the family, and a Shih Tzu in particular is such a "people dog" that the loss will seem even more acute when he is no longer sharing your home and life with you.

The best way of coming to terms with your loss is to talk to like-minded people. Reminisce with friends and family who knew your Shih Tzu, recounting all the good times you shared with your dog.

Your veterinarian may be able to recommend a good pet loss counseling service, and there are lots of dedicated sites on the Internet, where you can talk about how you feel, with other pet owners who know exactly what you are experiencing.

The sadness will never go away entirely, but it will lessen gradually with time, and, eventually, you will be able to think about your special Shih Tzu with a smile, instead of with tears.

FINAL FAREWELLS

June Weight from Saffron Walden, Essex, England has owned dogs for 40 years, 20 have been with Shih Tzus. She has had to say goodbye to many dogs in this time, but it is something which has never got any easier.

"My first Shih Tzu was Tanzie, who was the runt of the litter. She was always a very sickly dog – never robust and healthy – but, when she collapsed at the age of 11$\frac{1}{2}$, I knew something was seriously wrong. It was her liver. The veterinarian said 'Look, June, we can keep her going for another week or two, but she will still be in pain. You decide what we should do.' Of course, I had to have her put to sleep. It is a case of assessing the dog's quality of life. Tanzie wasn't going to live very much longer and was going to be in pain. What else could I decide?

"My first show Shih Tzu was Cassie. She was white-and-gold, and a very pretty, feminine dog. She was a born show-off, and was very laid-back in the ring. Cassie was 16$\frac{1}{2}$ when she started to become ill. She was a healthy dog, despite her age. She became blind, but adapted well, and was a little thin from old age, but otherwise was healthy, and was certainly enjoying life. It was when she had a stroke that I made the decision to have her put to sleep.

"From the stroke, her entire right side was paralyzed. This meant she had no independence at all. I had to carry her outside to go to the toilet. The Shih Tzu is a very noble breed, and I knew this wasn't fair. Cassie was a very proud little dog, and she would have hated to live like that. It was a hard decision to make, but I knew it was the right one.

SUDDEN SHOCK

"There have been times when I didn't have to decide to euthanize. Once, my husband took breakfast in to one of our male Shih Tzus, Aramis, and when he went back for the dish, he discovered the dog had died. Aramis had

Cassie: A proud dog who was allowed to end her life with dignity.

suffered a massive heart attack. It was an utter shock for us – we hadn't had a chance to say our goodbyes to him or anything – but for him, it was definitely the best way to die. He looked so peaceful, just as if he was asleep.

VETERINARY SUPPORT

"A very difficult loss was when Cherkara died in 1998. Cherkara developed cancer and we lost her at the age of seven. I felt robbed that we had lost her so early. The veterinarian got to know Cherkara, and myself, over the years, and she actually cried with me.

"Having an understanding, caring veterinarian is very important. In my veterinarian's practice no one is made to feel embarrassed for crying. The veterinarian understands that people will grieve because they have lost a good friend.

"Some people take their pets to the veterinarian and then leave them there to be put to sleep. I can't imagine doing that. Yes, it is hard, but imagine how the dog feels. I couldn't leave my friend there to die alone with strangers – I want to hold him to make him feel safe and loved. After everything they give to us, it's the least we can do for our animals."

CHAPTER SIX

BROADENING HORIZONS

The Shih Tzu is a bright, lively dog, that enjoys being busy. Yes, he will sit for hours on a warm lap, being cuddled and adored, but he will soon get very bored if this is all his life consists of. The Shih Tzu is an intelligent dog and needs to use his brain. Training is not only an ideal way of keeping your Shih Tzu's mind ticking, it is also a great way of spending quality time together and strengthening your relationship. There are lots of different canine sports and activities you can try – it's just a case of finding what best suits you both. Don't be discouraged by some of the sports, thinking a small dog won't be able to cope – the Shih Tzu is a big dog in a little body, who can certainly hold his own on an Agility course or in an Obedience ring. Never underestimate a Shih Tzu!

CANINE GOOD CITIZEN

The "Good Citizen" programs, organized by the American Kennel Club and the British Kennel Club, are an excellent starting point if you want to extend your dog's initial puppy training. The tests are designed to produce well-socialized canine citizens, who can behave appropriately in a number of everyday situations, such as:

- Accepting handling and grooming (essential for all dogs, but especially a coated breed like the Shih Tzu)
- Responding to basic obedience commands
- Meeting another dog
- Walking on a loose lead
- Walking confidently through a crowd of people
- Being approached and petted by a stranger.

Many of the exercises are already covered in Chapter Three, if your Shih Tzu needs to brush up on his training. Additionally, there are many participating training clubs in the United

Mary Baker with OTCH Itsy Bitsy Cookie Monster UDX.

Kingdom and the United States which help you to prepare your Shih Tzu for the tests. To find out more information on the programs, contact your national kennel club.

OBEDIENCE

The appearance of the glamorous Shih Tzu often belies the fact that the breed has brains as well as beauty. They aren't ditzy little bimbos capable only of lazing on laps all day (although they enjoy that too!); they also like to use their intelligence. Competitive Obedience provides this outlet.

Don't be fooled into thinking that Obedience is just for Border Collies. It is a fun sport that can be enjoyed by any breed, and at any level. Top-level Obedience holds certain obstacles for the Shih Tzu, who isn't built like the Collie. Heelwork turns won't be as fast as a Collie's,

for instance, but don't be discouraged. At every level of ability, Obedience is a fun way of sharing quality time with your dog.

It also has benefits in everyday life, helping to produce a well-mannered dog that you can trust in a variety of different situations. And, although it is tougher to reach the top, some Shih Tzus (such as the amazing OTCH Itsy Bitsy Cookie Monster, see page 87) are up there, giving the Collies and Golden Retrievers a good run for their money!

Voice of Experience

Bitsy's trainer, Mary Baker from Dallas, Texas, shares some of her training tips specially designed for Shih Tzus. Don't try the following until your Shih Tzu has accomplished the basic puppy obedience exercises in Chapter Three, pages 46-49.

Training Club

"There is much to be gained by working with a group, and I recommend that anyone interested in training, and possibly competing, finds a good group to train with.

"If I moved to a new location and wanted to find an instructor or group to train with, I would go to an Obedience trial in the area and watch the performances, then approach those handlers whose performances impressed me and find out where they train or if they teach classes. I would then see if I might observe classes before committing myself to a course of instruction. A good school and reasonable instructor should not object to this.

"I really like the more motivational techniques (reward-based training) being used today. There are many good techniques out there, but trying to incorporate them all will only make a mess of things. After deciding on a school, you should follow that instructor's method or he will be limited in what he can do for you. If you decide you would rather use another method, then go to a school that teaches that method.

Common Mistakes

"So often, I see dog and handler teams warming up outside the ring and they look so impressive, I am convinced they will be very high-scoring. However, when I watch their performance in the ring, it is often mediocre or worse. In my opinion, two mistakes (one training and one handling) account for most of this, and I have been guilty of both.

"The training mistake is to rely too heavily on treats. Many dogs can work beautifully when a treat is at hand, but soon learn that they don't get them in the ring. This happened with Bitsy, and she more or less shut down in the ring. I had to do extensive retraining to work through this, gradually weaning her away from instant gratification and convincing her that the reward would always be forthcoming – although randomly and eventually. Now she practically drags me out of the ring to get to her cookie box.

"The handling mistake is letting your nerves disconnect you from your dog. Handlers need to try to remain relaxed and communicate their encouragement and pleasure to their dog while in the ring. Their manner in the ring should be as much like it is in training as possible. I try to view each trial as a test to see where we might have improved, and what weaknesses need work, and to remember that no one trial is a do-or-die event. There's always another trial coming up, so relax and enjoy it.

Heeling

"The heel position is where the dog walks level with the handler's leg, neither in front nor behind, and close to the handler's leg. To teach heeling, I use a light leash or string leash, which I hold in my right hand, held at my right side, arm straight. The leash is draped across the front of my legs with about six inches of slack. The dog is placed on my left side. I hold a treat in my left hand at my left side, arm straight.

"As I walk, my left leg hits the leash in a manner that brings the dog in close and forward with me. I use my voice to encourage and praise his effort. As soon as I have the result I want, I give a command word ("Heel"), release him with an "Okay", and give him a treat and lots of praise.

"This method gives a natural, effective correction of the right degree, which dogs don't view in a negative way. The timing is correct without any effort from the handler, and the handler can concentrate on communicating with the dog.

"Once a good heelwork position has been achieved consistently, and the dog understands

the voice command and what is expected, move on to making turns. Work on gentle left-hand turns at first, moving on to sharper right-hand turns as the dog becomes more confident and able.

"Eventually, you should be able to work off-lead – and it should make no difference to the dog's performance. Don't rush any of these stages though, or you may undo all your hard work.

Stand From Down

"Put your dog in the Down position (page 48), with your treat-hand between his paws. To Stand your dog from this position, bring the treat-hand up and slightly forward, saying "Stand." If done properly, the dog will rise into a Stand without moving his feet. Keep practicing – you'll get there in the end!

Stand From Sit

"Put your dog in the Sit (page 47), by luring him with a treat. Then bring the treat up and forward slightly, saying "Stand" as you do so.

"It takes great practice to achieve the right position where the dog stands without losing his front leg placement. It may be worth putting something (such as a big book) in front of his feet, so that he cannot move forward. As before, practice makes perfect.

"All the positions (Stand from Down, Down from Stand, Stand from Sit and so on) should be alternated so the dog will learn to assume any of the positions from any of the other positions."

Mary Baker enjoys a challenge. A self-confessed dog lover, Mary set herself an extraordinary training test – to train one dog from each of the different dog groups to a title. It was this that first introduced her to the inimitable Bitsy, a Shih Tzu cookie monster, with an extraordinary flair for the sport.

"I have been in Obedience off and on for 40 years. A dog lover from an early age, I got my first AKC book of standards (published in 1945) when I was eight, and consider myself to be an all-breed fancier.

"I usually choose breeds not often seen in Obedience, and, at some point, decided to title a breed from each of the different dog groups. Breeds I have titled include, in order: UD Weimaraner (Sporting Dog); Ch. UD Pembroke Welsh Corgi (when still in the Working Group); CD Saluki (Hound); UD, WC Golden Retriever (Sporting); CD Greyhound (Hound); Ch. CD Bull Terrier (Terrier).

"Bitsy (OTCH Itsy Bitsy Cookie Monster UDX) is my first and only Shih Tzu – my breed of choice for the Toy group (Utility group in the United Kingdom). When I rescued her from a shelter in 1993, her age was estimated to be four or five years, which would make her 12 or 13 now. I started training her right away, and she got her Canine Good Citizen certificate four months later.

"Although I always try to get as good a representative of a breed as I can, and show in conformation if the dog has the potential for a Championship, my preferred interest has been Obedience. It has remained my primary dog activity through the years because of the close interaction between dog and owner, which has now reached a level comparable to dressage.

OVERCOMING PROBLEMS

"Shih Tzus are basically happy, perky, responsive, and forgiving little dogs. Bitsy is

The irrepressible Obedience Champion, Itsy Bitsy Cookie Monster UDX.

very routine-oriented, and can be willful and independent. I get around this by using consistent firmness – in everyday life as well as in training. For example, when out walking, Bitsy hates controls, so she gets to walk off-leash if she is responsive to me. If she gets willful, the lead is put back on.

"Food, toys and an eagerness to please are all used to motivate her. I view food and toys as tools to cultivate the eagerness to please, which I consider most desirable.

"Bitsy's first Novice show was a disaster. She was all over the ring, having a wonderful time at my expense. On the off-leash heeling, I lost her on the left turn. The judge called for a fast pace, and Bitsy raced to catch up. Then a normal, about-turn was called, and I lost her again. When she caught up, she started attacking my trouser legs and sat behind me when I stopped. I couldn't believe it. I had never misjudged a dog's readiness for the ring so badly.

"For a long time, she would really shake the glove on the Directed Retrieve. One time it flew out of her mouth about six feet straight up. When it came back down, she pounced on it and brought it back, wagging the glove from side to side in her mouth because of her speed. Another

THE REIGN OF THE COOKIE MONSTER ▶

time, after I had taken the glove from her, she jumped up and snatched it out of my hand.

RICH REWARDS

"What does Bitsy get out of Obedience? Primarily cookies (training treats). Dogs that have been on the streets often become food possessive, and Bitsy is obsessed with her cookies (as her Cookie Monster name suggests), which I have encouraged with much variety and escalating scrumptiousness. Her favorite homemade cookies are thin egg pancakes, with a wide variety of fillings, cut into thin strips. Her favorite filling is boiled, diced beef heart which I reserve for the shows. The treats motivate her to keep trying, but she is also enormously proud when she is told she has done a good job.

"Bitsy also enjoys the social aspects of going to class and to shows. My relationship with a dog that would bite me in a minute when I first got her has developed into a delightful rapport. One memorable moment was when a judge who had watched our performance from ringside one day said, 'You're a team now'.

"The breed tends to be sedentary and can sleep all day if allowed. I think the activity provided by regular training and showing has been good for Bitsy's health. It has boosted her confidence and has helped her to overcome some of her early bad experiences and behavior.

"My enjoyment in Obedience training and showing is derived from taking a breed that is quite rare in Obedience and seeing what I can do with it. Attitude is of paramount importance to me. What I think of the performance and what the spectators think have always meant more to me than what a judge's score reflects. Therefore, I don't need to win to be proud and happy. Sometimes a small improvement in a problem area or a single exercise done just the way I've been working to achieve will really thrill me. The wins eventually come as a by-product.

MAIN ATTRACTION

"I have been amazed at the notice Bitsy has attracted. Even when she is having a bad day, usually because of me, she still does enough of the performance in a style to bring admiration. I have had her stop during a heeling pattern three times and she has still gotten numerous compliments.

"When her confidence level is high, she is going full tilt for the most part, hair and tail flying, springing over jumps, sitting in front with her tail beating hard as if to say, 'What do you think of that? Wasn't that great?' Of course, she always thinks she's great, or at least deserving of a cookie!

Itsy Bitsy in action.
Photo courtesy: Donald Twynne.

"When Bitsy was placed third in the Toy Group at the 2000 AKC National Obedience Invitational, she started being talked about in the chat rooms on the Internet, and the president of the American Shih Tzu Club requested an article and photos. That was thrilling. Numerous Shih Tzu owners and exhibitors, both conformation and Obedience, have gone out of their way to be friendly and complimentary. There is so much competition and self-interest in dog activities that I have been really impressed by this, and very appreciative.

STAR OF THE SHOW

"We've come a long way since we started, and Bitsy now has an impressive track record. She was the number one Shih Tzu in 1999 and 2000 by two United States Obedience rating systems. She gained her UDX (Utility Dog Excellent) title in 1999, and qualified for the 2000 AKC National Obedience Invitational, winning 3rd place in the Toy Group. Bitsy's best all-breed Obedience trial win was when she was placed first in both Open B and Utility B the same day, with a 198.5 score (out of 200). She has a total of 30 UDX legs and has now earned her OTCH title (Obedience Trial Champion), which has been a great achievement.

TOUGH CUSTOMERS

"In my opinion, many people who get Shih Tzus seem to view them as fragile little toys and tend to spoil them into terrible tyrants. I view them as pretty tough customers that need an alpha leader as much as any dog. Many Shih Tzu owners need the guidance of a good Obedience school to help them mold their Shih Tzus into good citizens. Since they require considerable grooming, they need to learn to tolerate this. All dogs should be socialized with other dogs and with people, and training class is a good place to get this in a controlled atmosphere. The bonding that Obedience training promotes can only better the lives of both dog and owner."

AGILITY

Agility has become incredibly popular over the last few years, and it is easy to understand why. It can be enjoyed by any breed (and any owner), and is tremendous fun.

The aim of Agility is for each competitor to run through, over, up, down, or across a range of different obstacles as accurately and quickly as possible. The obstacles include:

- Hurdles: the dog must leap the hurdles, without knocking them.
- The long/broad jump: a series of elements laid on the ground, which the dog must clear.
- Tunnels: a collapsible canvas tunnel, and a rigid, open tunnel, which the dog must run through.
- Weaves: a series of poles fixed in the ground and set in a line. The dog must weave in and out of the poles.

Tackling the A-frame.

- See-saw/teeter: the dog must run up the see-saw, make it tip, and then run down.
- A-frame/ramp: an A-shaped obstacle, which the dog must run up and down.
- Dog walk: an elevated, narrow walkway, which the dog must cross.

The above three obstacles are classed as contact equipment, meaning the dog has to make contact with a marked area at the start and end of the obstacle. This not only ensures the dog's safety on otherwise potentially dangerous pieces of equipment, it also tests the handler's control and the dog's accuracy when working at speed.

Training

Training a Shih Tzu for Agility is best done through a club (contact your national kennel club for more information). There, you will receive thorough, safe tuition on the equipment. The classes are good fun, for dogs and owners alike, and nothing is rushed. Each obstacle is taught in simple steps, using rewards to encourage the dogs to cooperate.

Size Matters

Don't be discouraged from getting involved in Agility, thinking that your little Shih Tzu will never be able to leap the high hurdles that a Collie clears with ease. The height or breadth of the obstacle is determined by the size of the dog (see box, below).

Competitions

In the United Kingdom classes, all dogs compete against each other. They are allocated a position (first, second and so forth) according to their performance in relation to others in the class. All breeds compete together (within their size limits). This can make it difficult for a breed such as the Shih Tzu to excel in competitions, where he will be competing against faster, more athletic breeds.

AGILITY ORGANIZATIONS

In the United Kingdom, Agility is regulated by the Kennel Club. Shih Tzus qualify for the Mini-Agility class, where dogs must measure (at the shoulder) 1 foot, 3 inches (38.1 cm) or under. The maximum height for jumps is 1 foot, 3 inches (38.1 cm), except the tire jump, which is 1 foot, 8 inches (50.8 cm). The maximum distance for the long/broad jump is 2 feet, 6 inches (76.2 cm).

There are several types of Agility in the United States, each with slightly different regulations. With the AKC (American Kennel Club) and NADAC (North American Dog Agility Council), the A-frame is set lower at about 5 feet 6 inches (167.5 cm) and it has 8- and 12-inch (20- and 30.5-cm) jump heights.

In USDAA (United States Dog Agility Association), the A-frame is set at 6 feet, 3 inches (190.5 cms), and the lowest jump height is 12 inches (30.5 cm). The smaller Shih Tzu can have a lot of trouble with this.

In AKC Agility, dogs under 10 inches (25.5 cm) at the shoulder jump 8 inches (20 cm). This size jump is for dogs under 11 inches (28 cm) under NADAC Agility.

NADAC and USDAA also have a Veteran class for dogs over seven years of age; the jumps are dropped 4 inches (10 cm).

Phyllis Celmer, from Encinitas, California, has had Shih Tzus for more than 15 years. Previously a "big-dog" owner, she never wanted a small breed – until her sister-in-law adopted a Shih Tzu. From that moment on, Phyllis was enchanted, and, in her own words, "became obsessed by them!"

"I love the breed's self-confidence and sense of humor. They are big dogs in little bodies. I have five at the present time.

"I first became involved in Agility about seven years ago, when I entered one of my Shih Tzus – Kei Kei – at a dog show. I had just finished competing in the ring and decided to walk around the show grounds, when I noticed a lot of people gathered around one of the rings. There was quite a bit of laughter and applause, and I couldn't resist going over to see what all the commotion was about.

"The local Agility club was putting on a demonstration and it was quite a hit with everyone, including me. I thought it was

Phyllis Celmer coaches Kei Kei down the A-frame.

something that Kei Kei would enjoy working at. Kei Kei has always been a handful; she is very lively and full of energy, and she had become bored with Obedience and showing. It was time for a change.

"In our first Agility class, there were quite a few big-dog owners and I was teased about my 'dustmop.' They wanted to know if she was there to clean off the equipment! Well, we showed them – Kei Kei was the first dog in her class to get a qualifying leg and the first to title in Agility. Kei Kei is now approaching 10 years of age, and is still running. Recently, she gained her first leg for her Master's titles, and already has her Elite titles with NADAC.

"Kei Kei has been joined by Taz, who is now four years old – and both dogs have their Agility Excellent titles, Standard, and Jumpers with Weaves. Taz is also half-way to both of his Master titles. So, tell me Shih Tzus can't do Agility!

"I got Taz when he was four months old. I started with some basic showing and fun Obedience training, and we moved him on to more formal Agility training at six months. He has now been involved in the sport for three and a half years. Taz was Top Shih Tzu in Agility for 1998 and 2000, for both the American Shih Tzu Club and the American Kennel Club (Kei Kei was top in the ASTC in 1996).

STUBBORN STUDENTS

"Shih Tzus can sometimes be temperamental during training. It's not that they don't want to do it, they just don't want to be told to do it. But it's pretty easy to fix. I just put the dog back in the house and work with the other one. No dog wants to be left out, and they do come around quickly – trust me, this works!

"Taz is my little 'brat-boy' some days. He does not like to run

THE FLYING DUSTBUSTERS ▶

when it's too warm, and has been known to lie under the A-frame, or leave the ring to visit his adoring fans. This can be truly frustrating – especially when he's had a perfect run going, and, with only one obstacle to go, he disappears!

"Usually if an error is made, though, it's due to the handler. I think the female Shih Tzu is less forgiving than the male. You should see some of the looks I've received from Kei Kei when I've messed up! Most of the female Shih Tzus that I've seen running are all more intense than the male dogs, and are generally faster.

STARS OF THE SHOW

"People love watching my little dogs and they are surprised to see Shih Tzus compete in Agility. In the beginning, when he was in full show coat, it was awesome to watch Taz jumping, but once he finished with his show career, I trimmed him down. It was too much work to keep him in full coat.

"Our biggest enemy is time. It is hard for the Shih Tzu to make good time. Small dogs are allowed an extra five seconds, and you can still qualify with some time faults, but it is preferable to have a 'clean run.' I'm always working with my dogs on building speed, whether through faster entries into the weavepoles, or a continuous movement on the teeter (see-saw) or A-frame to shave off a few seconds. Getting my Shih Tzus down from the A-frame can sometimes be difficult – they love to perch up high!

TEAM WORK

"Kei Kei and Taz love Agility. It's a major feat trying to get out of the house on the morning of a show! I keep my training shoes in the car now – I can't put them on in the house, as the dogs knock me over; they have no patience at all. As soon as they realize where we're going (it doesn't take long, no matter how sneaky I try to be), they get so excited.

"For me, Agility is pure enjoyment. I'm not sure when and where it happens, but you and your dog learn to work as a team. As you learn to develop correct handling techniques, and they learn to read your body movements, it all starts to come together.

Fur flying, Taz takes the hurdles in his stride.

Dogs love Agility, and Taz shows he is no exception.

"Some people still think Shih Tzus cannot be trained for Agility, but a dog is only as smart as its owner. My dogs are professional students: they start with conformation training, Obedience, trick classes, Agility classes, and, if we didn't have so many coyotes here, probably Tracking classes (coyotes usually attack small wild animals, but they get caught in neighborhoods in the canyons and will also attack small domestic animals such as cats and small dogs).

"You have to know and understand your breed; only then can you start to enjoy your dogs to the fullest. Shih Tzus are ideal for Agility: they love to run, climb, jump and learn, and are very clever little characters. The more you teach your dogs, the more they want to learn.

"Shih Tzus can have their moments and they do sometimes have a bit of an attitude, but if they didn't, they wouldn't be Shih Tzus! When they are wonderful, they are wonderful, and when they are bad, they are naughty brats!"

In the United States, competitors do not really compete against each other. There are placings from 1st through to 4th, but they are not the be-all and the end-all, as competitors are more interested in qualifying. If ten dogs are entered in a class, they could all qualify or none could qualify, according to whether the course is completed in a set time and a set score is obtained. When you receive three qualifying scores, you get a title for that class and can move up to the next category.

CONFORMATION SHOWING

The show world can be a daunting place to the novice, full of rules and regulations, and strange terminology. At first, it might seem that everyone knows each other, everyone has perfectly groomed and well-behaved dogs, and no one would give your Shih Tzu a second glance – but this is not necessarily the case. The show world is generally a friendly one, and a new face soon attracts amiable Shih Tzu fans who will be more than happy to chat and give you advice.

First Step

Before you consider showing, you must have a dog that is worthy of being exhibited, and that is registered with your national kennel club. If you did not request a show-quality puppy, from respected parents, then you will need to ask the advice of your dog's breeder, who will be able to give you an honest assessment of your dog. If your dog won't make the grade, why not consider entering fun shows? They are very enjoyable events, and make a good day out.

Davis Crossley and his wife, Susan, have always liked to be a little different. The first dog they had after they married was a Great Dane, Spartan, whom they attempted to show. Unfortunately, he had a number of faults which meant his career in the ring never really took off. Because David and Susan didn't have the room for another Great Dane, they looked around for a smaller breed, and their taste for the exotic led them to the Shih Tzu.

"Thirty years ago, the Shih Tzu was not very well known," says David from Crewe, Cheshire, England. "We saw a photo of a Shih Tzu, and liked the look of him. The more we researched the breed, the more it appealed to us – especially the dogs' happy-go-lucky attitude.

"Our first Shih Tzu was Timothy (Oakwood Golden Falcon). He was a promising puppy, but never developed into a show-quality dog. He was a great pet, though, and got on really well with Spartan.

"It all went from there, really; we took on more dogs, and learned a lot from ring-training classes and from other people. You never stop learning. Thirty years later, we're still learning new things.

NERVOUS ENERGY
"The first few times you go into the ring, it can be terrifying. When we started, there weren't as many Shih Tzus being shown as there are now, but there were some big names that won time after time. You'd go into the ring, and look around, and think 'Oh, heck; we'll never beat them.' But you get more confident with practice, and learn what makes a good dog.

THE BIG TIME
"The first big success we had was with Santosha Rambling Rose (pet name, Brandy), who was from the first litter we ever bred. We took a lot of advice when planning the litter, and, as the puppies were growing, everyone picked out the same puppy as having the most potential. We

Ch. Santosha Stromboli.

kept this puppy, and gave Brandy to Sue's parents as a thank you for helping out with the litter. Brandy would come to us regularly to be bathed and groomed, and, when she was about 18 months old, and we had finished grooming her, we looked at her, then looked again – it was just like the proverbial ugly duckling who had developed into a swan!

"We started showing Brandy. Often we would pick her up from Sue's parents on the Friday evening, and she would be full of briars from having been out rabbit hunting with Sue's dad, and then we would have to get her ready for a show the following day!

"Brandy was a really sound mover. She was in great shape due to all the walking and rabbit hunting she did, and, although she was very pretty, she wasn't a glamour girl – she was really sound.

GOING FOR GOLD

"Brandy's first Challenge Certificate came as a real surprise to a lot of people, especially as it was given by an eminent judge in the breed.

In the early days, the feeling you get of winning a CC is similar to how you imagine people feel when they win gold at the Olympics!

"A year later, Brandy had won a second CC and I was handling her at Crufts. Sue, who usually handles the dogs, was in the hospital, so it was up to me.

There, she won Best of Breed under the renowned breed specialist, Audrey Dadds. I nearly missed going into the Group competition because I had to telephone Sue in the hospital to tell her to watch it on television. That day was a very special one for us, and it actually brought tears to my eyes.

"Brandy was an excellent case for showing people that the Shih Tzu shouldn't be wrapped up in cotton, or caged to protect the coat. It's much more important that they are happy in life.

GOOD BREEDING

"For us, breeding and showing go hand in hand. There is nothing better than to breed your own puppy, to watch it mature through puppy class into adulthood, and then to see it win. The planning of that dog begins well before its conception, when you assess your line and start looking at possible dogs to complement it. Even if you breed a puppy and it goes to someone else, it is still a great feeling when they do well. It means you have produced something good, that has contributed to the future of the breed. All too often, people concentrate too much on winning, and forget that, really, it is all about the breed's well-being.

SUCCESS STORY

"Since Brandy, our Santosha kennel has had considerable success. We don't keep a tally of the number of Champions we've had – numbers are not that important to us – but there have been many. The highlights include winning the Best Dog CC at Crufts for two years running, a number of Best of Breeds at Championship shows, and, one year, winning the Best Bitch and Best Dog at Crufts.

The current dog we are campaigning is Santosha Stromboli (pictured). He has won Best Dog at Crufts for two years running, and has also been named top-winning Shih Tzu.

"Stromboli won his first CC aged around 14 months and was a Champion before he was two years. He's four now, and is a great little dog. In the ring, he's clever and easy-going; at home, he's a lovely individual too – he must have a cuddle with us before he goes to bed, or he won't settle!

"Sue and I have judged at Championship level all over the world, and I'm chairman of the Shih Tzu Club, so it's fair to say that, from what started as a hobby, Shih Tzus have become a central part of our lives now – very much a full-time job."

Every dog is given a thorough "hands-on" examination by the judge.

If your dog is a show-quality specimen, good enough to compete at sanctioned events, then you should enroll at your nearest ring-training class (ask your kennel club for details). There, your Shih Tzu will socialize with other dogs, and learn how to behave in the ring. You will be taught ring procedure, how to present your dog to his best advantage, and how to gait (move) him. Help and advice from experienced show people is available.

Stacking

Stacking is the art of presenting the dog for the judge's assessment. Being a small breed, the Shih Tzu is posed on a table. The dog must appear well balanced, with the legs placed straight. The head is held fairly high (emphasising the impression of haughtiness), and the tail should fall over the back. It is acceptable to hold the head and tail in the correct position if the dog does not do so of his own accord – though most learn what is expected of them with practice.

Good socialization from an early age should mean your Shih Tzu will have no qualms about being handled by unfamiliar people (i.e., judges) – see Chapter Three.

Gaiting

A well-structured Shih Tzu on the move is simply a joy to watch. The movement of the coat, the rear driving action, and the characteristic "arrogance and style" is truly an impressive sight. But it is not achieved overnight! It takes practice and experience to move well as a pair, and to learn the right gait for your individual dog. Attend as many shows as you can, as a spectator, to watch how others gait their Shih Tzus. This should give you some tips for when you practice with your dog.

Becoming a Champion

In Britain, a dog must win three Challenge Certificates (CCs) under three different judges at three different shows in order to qualify as a Champion.

In the United States, a dog must gain 15 points at licensed shows. The maximum number of points offered at a show are five, so a Shih Tzu must win points at a minimum of three shows and under three different judges. The 15 points must be made up of at least two "majors," which are awards of three, four or five points.

CHAPTER SEVEN

A SPECIAL BOND

Although considered a supreme companion dog, happy to sit on a lap being adored for hours on end, the Shih Tzu is much, much more than just a pretty face. As any owner will tell you, these dogs are highly intelligent. They are also "busy" little creatures, that like to be kept occupied – in mind as well as in body.

Fortunately, there are numerous activities in which Shih Tzus and their owners can take part (Chapter Six). A select few, however, have demanding careers as therapy and assistance (service) dogs, roles which enable them to combine their love of people with their love of learning.

THERAPY DOGS

Numerous studies have proved that humans who have contact with pets benefit both physically and psychologically. This news comes as no surprise to pet owners, who know how much better they feel after interacting with their pet on a bad day.

For dog owners who have to spend time in the hospital or in a residential home, lack of contact with animals can have a detrimental effect. For many, moving into these establishments is a stressful, anxious time – the very time when they most need the comfort of a pet. Unfortunately, most places have a no-pets policy.

Thanks to a committed band of volunteers, however, residents and patients can enjoy all the benefits of pet ownership without the full-time responsibility. Programs are in place in Britain and the United States, where owners can take their well-behaved dogs to visit people in a range of different establishments – including schools, hospitals, hospices, and homes for the elderly, as well as going to see children and adults with learning disabilities.

The Shih Tzu is a popular therapy dog, thriving on attention and human contact. Plus, he is small enough to fit on a lap, and has an appealing face (who can resist those eyes?), and a long, luxurious coat that is a pleasure to stroke.

LADY SADIE

Tammy Marshall from Lubbock, Texas, has worked with people with learning difficulties for more than 13 years. In therapy dog work, she has found the ideal way to combine her two passions in life – her work and her dogs.

"I have always wanted to spend the most time I can with my dogs – Sadie, a Shih Tzu, and Shelby and Tory, my Tibetan Terriers. I work with people who have learning difficulties, and I realized how much these people could benefit from being around animals. Many have never had contact with pets and are unable to express themselves or show affection. I thought therapy work could help them show affection appropriately, as well as to bond with a living creature that loved them unconditionally.

Sadie with Tammy Marshall: Working together they spread a feeling of happiness.

"Through some research I learned of the power that pet therapy has on individuals. This, together with my love for dogs and my desire to work with people with learning difficulties, got me interested in pet therapy work.

"I took Sadie through some basic obedience classes, as well as a Canine Good Citizen class. She then had to take the CGC Test and Therapy Dog evaluation test. Once those were completed and her health check was done, she was eligible for therapy work, which she started at the grand age of seven. Sadie has since received more Obedience training and earned her Companion Dog (CD) title.

"I currently visit a school and a local hospital and I try to go as often as I can. Sadie is ideal for therapy dog work because she loves people and being the center of attention. She is outgoing, happy, and affectionate, and is a wonderful companion, though, like many Shih Tzus I know, she can be stubborn.

LAP DOG

"Sadie believes her place in life is on the lap of anyone who will pet and love her. If she is not on someone's lap, she tries to gain their attention by dancing or sitting up. She loves people of all ages and has never met a stranger that she didn't like.

"Sadie's size is an asset in therapy dog work, as she only weighs 10 pounds. This enables her to sit on people's laps or on the bed next to them, without causing pain or distress to them.

"Most people's faces light up when Sadie enters the room, and a smile quickly follows. Some have been timid or a little frightened just because Sadie is a dog, but she wins them over in no time at all, and she is soon on their lap or bed being petted. Many also open up and begin talking about their own loved pets.

"One of the individuals we have visited was very weak and fragile. When he

LADY SADIE ▶

LADY SADIE

Sadie loves being the center of attention.

saw Sadie for the first time, he began pointing his finger at her and saying 'dog.' He said several words that day and in subsequent visits. The staff were very excited about this, as he had not said a word since he was admitted. They were amazed that he knew any words at all, and said that Sadie had opened up a new world for them and for him.

"Through our visits, people who are behaviorally challenged learn to take turns, to be gentle, and to show affection appropriately. At first, I had one individual who was very scared of dogs. In a matter of weeks, she was running out to meet me when we arrived. This individual hardly ever smiled or showed enjoyment, yet, in time, she was laughing and smiling just at the sight of Sadie.

"One night, when visiting in the hospital, I was asked to see an elderly woman who had been very depressed, as no one had been to visit her in weeks. I went into the room with Sadie, and the woman began to cry. She kept saying over and over that it meant so much that I would take the time to visit, and that we had made her day. Every time I think of this, I get tears in my eyes.

CHILDREN'S FRIEND

"When visiting children, they can be tearful and scared sometimes. The sight of Sadie stops that almost instantly, and they begin laughing and smiling. Sadie is able to calm them down if they are anxious, and makes their time in hospital less scary.

"I remember one visit when the mother of a crying toddler motioned for me to come to her daughter's bed. She said that she didn't know how her daughter would respond, but she had tried everything to make the child happy, with no success, and wanted to see if Sadie could help.

"Once the little girl saw Sadie, she immediately stopped crying and looked at her. Within a few minutes, Sadie was on the bed and the toddler was petting her and laughing. This has happened on more than one occasion with other children. The mother was amazed and couldn't thank me enough for changing her daughter's mood and calming her.

RAY OF SUNSHINE

"It's not just the patients who benefit from our visits. Hospitals can be very anxious times for relatives, too. One time, we visited the waiting room where families were waiting for news of how their loved ones had coped in surgery. The packed room was very gloomy and quiet.

"In a matter of minutes, Sadie had changed the

atmosphere. Many of the people started talking about why they were there, and about their own dogs. Many started to pet Sadie and soon their demeanor was a little less stressed; some even laughed at the sight of Sadie dancing and sitting up to get their attention. One family later told me that even after we had left, people continued to talk about their dogs, and how Sadie's visit was a nice break in all they were dealing with.

"Sadie improves people's lives in many ways. She brightens up the lives of those in the hospital who may be going through a difficult time. Many patients long to hold their own pets, and seeing or petting Sadie helps them work towards a faster recovery so they can get back to their beloved pets at home. For people who do not have pets, Sadie provides a chance to see what the love of a pet can do, and she is a brilliant ambassador for dogs in general, showing how loving and well behaved they can be.

REWARDING WORK

"Sadie adores her visits. She gets all the love and attention that she so enjoys. She also likes showing off and worming her way into the hearts of others. Just the sound of me picking up her collar with her Therapy Dog tag on gets Sadie so excited that she races towards the door. Once in the car, she sits calmly until we reach our destination and then she becomes so excited that she whines or barks in sheer joy. That in itself tells me she loves what she does.

"I look forward to our therapy visits too. It is always so rewarding. When I leave, at the end of a session, I have a new sense of myself and feel honored that Sadie and I have made a difference in someone else's life. No matter what my mood is before going, it is always so much better after I finish. Therapy work gives the opportunity to spend time with my dogs, sharing their unconditional love for life with others."

HEARING DOGS

The work of guide dogs, or "Seeing Eye" dogs, is well known around the world, but far fewer people are aware of the work of hearing dogs, animals that act as the ears for deaf people or those who have severely impaired hearing. Unlike guide dogs, much smaller breeds can be employed as hearing dogs, and several Shih Tzus (and many Shih Tzu crosses) have been successfully trained for the job.

"People are extremely surprised, not to mention shocked, to see Shih Tzu hearing dogs," explains Lisa Wigmore, from Hearing Dogs for Deaf People in Britain. "We train dogs of all shapes and sizes – purebreeds, crossbreeds and mixed breeds. As more hearing dogs are being placed, people are beginning to realize that they are not all Labradors!

"The Shih Tzus that we have trained have shown themselves to be very self-assured little dogs," Lisa continues. "This makes them ideal to be placed in homes where the owners lead fairly busy lives, as the dogs take everything in their stride. This confidence, combined with a calm, steady temperament and small size, has made them very easy to place – even with recipients who are not necessarily experienced with dogs."

Of course, grooming is an important consideration when matching a Shih Tzu to an owner, and any deaf recipient must consider it a relaxing pastime to groom a long-haired dog. The option is given for the recipient to keep the dog's coat clipped.

GLITZY RITZY

Life, for Rita Bradley from London, had become quite a hopeless affair. Her deafness made her feel isolated from the rest of the world, and she became lonely and depressed – until Ritzy came along . . .

"I used to be a fun-loving, outgoing party girl," explains Rita. "I was a model and actress in the 1960s. I mixed with aristocracy, actors, singers and pop groups, and life was very exciting indeed. But everything started to change when I became ill.

"At first, I began to miss out on words people said, and then I started keeling over. Sometimes, I would wake up completely deaf. The doctors were at a complete loss as to what was wrong with me, and it was several years before I was diagnosed as having Ménières, a stress-related nerve deafness disorder. It affects balance as well as hearing, and often I look drunk when I haven't even touched a glass of water. It is rarely bilateral, but my luck being what it is, both my ears are affected.

DESPAIR AND HOPE

"It is very difficult to lose your hearing in adult life. I missed music dreadfully, and couldn't learn sign language (it is so different grammatically). I felt in some kind of no-man's-land between the deaf and non-deaf worlds, belonging to neither.

"I became very depressed because of my hearing difficulties and on more than one occasion even tried to take my own life.

Rita Bradley with Ritzy – the love of her life.

"In the hospital, my neurootologist asked me to consider having a hearing dog. I have always been interested in animals, and have owned numerous cats and dogs. When Hearing Dogs For Deaf People came around to assess me, I told them I had owned Shih Tzus and Yorkies before, and went on the waiting list.

"A few months later, I received a letter asking if I would be interested in Ritzy, a Shih Tzu that had just finished her initial training. They sent a photo of her. As soon as I saw her, I just burst into tears. At once, I felt as if I could live again. I cried and cried and cried – not from self-pity, but from relief.

"When I first met her, she had just been shampooed; she looked and smelled gorgeous. She ran straight to me, and I picked her up and kissed her and cuddled her. Since then, she has been the love of my life. Without her, I would be nothing.

HAPPY NEW YEAR

"At night, when my hearing-aid is not in, I can hear nothing, and Ritzy acts as my ears, alerting me to any danger. Even with my hearing-aid in, she helps me all the time. She tells me if someone is at the door, if the phone is ringing, if the alarm is going off – all the time, she acts as my ears.

"Fireworks drive her crazy, as she alerts me every time one goes off, and can't understand why they continue (sounds such as the telephone or doorbell usually stop when she alerts me). On Millennium Eve, she had to be sedated to stop her getting too upset by the explosions.

"I didn't get to sleep until very late that night. Then, a few hours later, I felt the bed moving. I thought I was dreaming, but then I realised Ritzy was taking the covers off me and had started to pull at my hair! I thought she wanted to go outside to piddle, so I stumbled out of bed to let her out.

"I was dead to the world – in a real daze. Then I saw the real reason why Ritzy had been so desperate to wake me up – there was a man coming over the fence. I shouted at him, and Ritzy went out there as if she was a Rottweiler – she is such a gutsy lady. She has a very deep bark for a little dog, and sounds much fiercer than she is.

"The closed-circuit television revealed there were two guys trying to break in. I had a lucky escape thanks to Ritzy, especially as I realized that I hadn't locked the door to the house. Even the police said how clever she was. She is so good at her job.

"Ritzy's not my ears, she's my right arm, my lifeblood, and the bond between us is incredible. She gives me a purpose in life. If I am ill, I have to get up to let her outside. If I feel dizzy, she will gently lick and reassure me. She's my best friend, and keeps me from being so alone. Without her, I'd be like a ghost."

Ritzy seems to sense when Rita is in trouble.

A FRIEND TO MANY

Naomi Frankfort is a 79-year-old from Silver Spring, Maryland, who lost her hearing six years ago. Thanks to Shayna, her five-year-old Shih Tzu, Naomi can once again lead a full and happy life.

"I have always loved dogs, and have owned a Boxer, a terrier, a Cocker Spaniel, and several mixed breeds. Shayna is my first Shih Tzu. I researched the breed thoroughly prior to purchasing Shayna. I wanted a dog that was small, and was suited to family life (I have lots of grandchildren). Of all the dogs my family has owned, Shayna is the most adorable and lovable, and probably the most intelligent. I can highly recommend the breed as a wonderful family pet or as a hearing dog.

LIFE-CHANGING EXPERIENCE

"Shayna has changed my life completely. I retired from teaching elementary school pupils in 1980 and did a great deal of volunteer work until about six years ago when I suddenly lost most of my hearing due to a blood condition. I am now considered severely to profoundly deaf, and totally deaf without my hearing-aids.

"My husband, Jesse, and I used to attend the theater, go to restaurants and enjoy many social events, but having a hearing loss made that difficult and I started to remain at home all the time, becoming quite depressed. It was then that we decided to get a dog since we were at home so much.

"Shayna was 12 weeks old when I was told of the Hearing Dog Training Center in Florida where we lived at the time. It took six months of weekly sessions to train and certify her as a hearing dog. Usually, hearing dog recipients are given a trained dog, rather than training their own dogs, but Shayna is a rare case.

"Her work is very varied. When the alarm goes off in the morning, she wakes me by jumping on the bed and nibbling on my fingers. She gets me

Naomi Frankfort with Shayna: Now Naomi can live a full and rewarding life.

and takes me to the door when the doorbell rings or when the smoke alarm sounds. She does so much it is difficult to remember it all – she lets me know when the microwave bell rings, when someone sounds a car horn, and of any unusual sounds inside the house or outside.

"Shayna is so well behaved in public. She can lie at my side for an hour while we wait for a doctor's appointment, and then she will jump to attention and alert me when my name is called. She also knows Jesse's name. When I ask her to get him, she jumps up on him and takes him to me.

CHILD AT HEART

"Shayna is something of a performer. She accompanies me when I speak to large groups of senior citizens about hearing loss and how to cope with the disability. Shayna shows how she helps me so that I am no longer disabled by the loss of my hearing. We also speak to elementary school children about preserving their hearing. Shayna loves to attend these meetings as she adores children. She still thinks that she is a puppy when children are around. She loves to play and is exceptionally gentle with them, softly licking their fingers if they ask for a kiss.

HEARTWARMING

"I have experienced several very emotional and touching moments while working with Shayna. In Florida, while visiting a nursing home (to bring a little cheer to those residents who are confined to bed and rarely have visitors), there was a woman confined to a wheelchair who hadn't spoken since she arrived at the home several weeks before.

"The nurse who was taking me around informed me that the woman was French and did not speak English. Although I had studied French in college, it had been many years since I had used the language. I started to speak to her and introduced Shayna and myself. At first, she responded with a nod of her head and then, to our delight, began to speak. As she took Shayna into her lap, we all had tears in our eyes.

CAREER GIRL

"People are often surprised to see such a small service dog. She wears the orange collar, vest and leash that signifies a service animal and wears tags that say 'Service Dog.' Shayna has a golden head with a section of white on the top – she looks like vanilla ice cream with butterscotch swirl! I am stopped wherever I go as people remark that she is a most beautiful dog, with an outstandingly intelligent face. They are often amazed that she is a working dog. Most people have never heard of hearing dogs.

"Shayna is exceptionally well trained and responds at once to all commands, including hand signals. She has become much more than a friend – she sleeps in our bed and always makes us laugh before going to sleep. In the morning, she brings us her toys and starts our day once again with smiles and laughter. When I want to work quietly on my computer, she sits right next to me for as long as I am busy.

"Shayna has more than lived up to my expectations – she has become the delight of our lives."

CHAPTER EIGHT

SEEKING PERFECTION

Every recognized breed of dog has a Breed Standard, a written blueprint which describes the ideal specimen of each breed. Everything from the dog's temperament, coat, and physical structure are described – from the color of the nose to the carriage of the tail.

Some breeds have slightly different Breed Standards according to the registration body. For example, the American Kennel Club has a slightly different Standard for the Shih Tzu than the Kennel Club in Britain, although they agree on all the key points.

In the show ring, the Breed Standard is the guide by which a judge assesses each competitor. It is the dog that is closest to the ideal described in the Standard that wins. This means that the best winners – those that are sought after for breeding or for work at stud – are instrumental in the future of the breed, passing on their sound characteristics to other generations.

SUMMARY OF STANDARDS

Many of the points in the Breed Standard relate to the breed's history and its original function – that of a companion dog in Tibet. The following is a précis of the key points of the American and British Breed Standards, and explains why the breed is constructed as it is.

General appearance

Although small and glamorous, the Shih Tzu should not appear fragile, like a Yorkshire Terrier, for example. Rather, he should be sturdy and compact, with a proud, arrogant carriage. This characteristic sense of haughtiness befits the Shih Tzu's links with the imperial court. The breed's most distinctive feature is the long and abundant coat.

Characteristics

The Shih Tzu is intelligent and lively. An alert attitude is a hallmark of the breed.

Temperament

The Shih Tzu is friendly, happy, and affectionate, as befits a companion dog. The British Standard also emphasises the breed's independence.

Head and skull

The head should be broad, round, and wide between the eyes. These features are linked with neoteny, meaning they are characteristics seen in babies. Dogs bred solely as companion dogs often have these features, to make them even more appealing to humans.

The Shih Tzu face is frequently described as being "chrysanthemum-like," thanks to the breed's facial hair growing outwards in all directions.

The muzzle should be square, short, smooth (unwrinkled) and flat. The nose should be about 1 inch (2.5 cms) from its tip to a well-defined stop (the indentation between the eyes). It should be level, or slightly tilted upwards (contributing to the impression of haughtiness), but never down-turned. The nostrils should be wide and open. This ensures that the dog receives maximum oxygen, especially important in a breed with a "squashed nose," which originated in a country of extreme temperatures and in high altitudes.

The nose color should be black, except in liver dogs, when the nose should also be liver. In the American Standard, a blue nose or lighter-colored nose is also acceptable in blue-pigmented dogs.

Eyes

Emphasizing the dog's "baby appeal," the eyes should be large, dark, round, and placed well apart. A lighter shade is allowed in liver-colored dogs, or those with liver markings. The eye rims should be the same pigment as the nose.

The head is broad and round; the eyes are large, dark and round.

Ears

The ears should be long and large. Set just below the crown, they are so abundantly coated that they are difficult to distinguish from the dog's neck hair.

The long, pendulous ears are another feature of neoteny – as nearly all breeds have droopy ears, before they become erect as the puppy matures into adulthood. The fact that the Shih Tzu is a companion dog means he does not need pricked ears to pick up sounds, as a working dog would require. Hence, the ears can be heavily coated – and all the better to stroke.

Mouth

The mouth should be broad and wide. The bite should be undershot (the lower teeth slightly overlapping the upper teeth), although a level bite (where the lower and upper teeth meet edge to edge) is permissible in Britain.

A missing tooth or slightly misaligned teeth are not heavily penalized in the United States, presumably because they have little importance in the breed's function. A companion dog cannot be compared to a gundog, for example, that relies on his teeth to retrieve game.

Neck

The Shih Tzu's neck should be in proportion to the rest of the dog's body – of sufficient length to allow the dog to hold his head proudly, but not too long. The neck should arch slightly, flowing naturally into the dog's shoulders.

Forequarters

The shoulders are well laid back and well angulated. The legs are short, muscular and straight. Some people do not expect the Shih Tzu to be as muscular as he is, but remember, this is not a fragile little Toy dog, but a robust, big dog in a small body.

Body

The Shih Tzu is slightly longer than he is tall. His body should be sturdy (differentiating him from the tiny Toy breeds), with a broad, deep chest, that provides good lung room – essential in a brachycephalic (short-nosed breed).

The Shih Tzu topline (the line of the back) should be level, and the dog should be short-coupled, meaning he should have a definite "waist."

Hindquarters

Like the forelegs, the well-rounded hindlegs should be muscular and straight (when viewed from behind). The abundance of hair makes the rear legs look much larger than they actually are.

Feet

The feet are round, and the pads are firm. This is important in the breed, because the hair can clump between the pads, so the pads need to be strong. The pads would have acted as strong, effective 'snowboots' in his native country. Like the rear legs, the feet appear to be much larger than they actually are thanks to the profusion of hair.

Tail

Like the rest of the hirsute Shih Tzu, the tail is heavily plumed. It is placed fairly high, level with the dog's head, in order to balance the dog's overall shape. The tail is carried "gaily" over the dog's back in a curve.

Gait/movement

The Shih Tzu should move smoothly and effortlessly, but this is certainly not a breed that floats effortlessly around the ring – he emits a real sense of power when he moves – the forelegs reaching well forward, and with a good drive from the rear. The overall impression should be one of arrogance, with the dog holding his head high.

Coat

This is the Shih Tzu's crowning feature. The

Movement is seemingly effortless, with the forelegs reaching forward and good drive from the rear.

coat should be long and abundant. A slight wave is allowed, but in no way should it be curly. The undercoat should be as profuse as the topcoat. A double coat would have been essential in a breed native to Tibet, a country with extremely cold winters. And a warm lap dog usually meant a warm lap for the dog's owner!

The long hair on top of the head is tied in a topknot to keep the hair away from the eyes – and to show off the dog's adorable little face!

All coat colors are permissible – including black, gold, brindle, gray, liver, silver, and sometimes blue, and blue-and-white (although this color is not very common). All these colors can be combined with white.

It is easier to see the strong, striding action of the Shih Tzu in this clipped dog.

In the United Kingdom, a white tip on the tail or a blaze (patch of white) on the forehead is highly desirable in parti-colored dogs (those with patches of two or more colors).

Size

In the United Kingdom, the Shih Tzu should measure no more than $10^1/_2$ inches (26.7 cm) from the ground to the withers (shoulder). In the United States, the ideal height is stated as 9 to $10^1/_2$ inches (22.8 to 26.7 cm), with 8 inches (20.3 cm) being the absolute minimum size, and 11 inches (27.9 cm) being the absolute maximum. There is no minimum size in the United Kingdom, although most exhibitors remember the phrase "not a Toy nor a terrier" that used to appear in the Standard, but which is now removed. Tiny Shih Tzus, therefore, are very rarely seen.

The British Standard suggests a weight band of 10 to 18 pounds (4.5 to 8.1 kg), with the ideal weight being between 10 and 16 pounds (4.5 to 7.3 kg). The American Breed Standard stipulates a slightly lower weight, giving 9 to 16 pounds (4 to 7.3 kg) as the ideal weight range.

BREEDING

If you have a purebred Shih Tzu that is registered with your national kennel club, you will have a pedigree for your dog. This is a genealogy chart listing the dog's recent ancestors. At first glance, this can look confusing, but, like a human family tree, this is a fascinating document which will give you a valuable insight into your dog and his breeding.

There are three ways of breeding dogs:

• Inbreeding, where very close relations, such as

father and daughter, are bred together

- Linebreeding, where more distant relations, such as those that share the same grandfather, are used
- Outcrossing, where unrelated dogs are mated together.

Inbreeding is rarely used in Shih Tzus as it can cause many health problems and faults if carried out by novice breeders. It is far better to use linebreeding to "fix" a type, and then to use outcrossing periodically to bring in fresh blood and desirable characteristics, and to prevent the line becoming too concentrated.

From your dog's pedigree, you can tell the type of breeding program that was used. In an outcross dog, the sire (at the top half of the pedigree) and the dam (at the bottom half) will share none of the same ancestors. In a linebred dog, some names or kennel affixes will recur.

FROM PUPPY TO CHAMPION

A Shih Tzu puppy looks very different from an adult dog, and there is no way of predicting for certain whether an eight-week-old puppy will develop into a successful show dog (although viewing the parents gives some indication).

Some promising puppies fail to live up to expectations, perhaps becoming too large, developing the wrong dentition, or lacking the profuse coat that is required for the show ring. Or maybe the dog does not have the correct temperament for being exhibited – perhaps being too shy or introverted. Sometimes, unprepossessing puppies who look quite ordinary at eight weeks blossom into breathtaking beauties. Here is how one Shih Tzu puppy developed into a Champion.

A pedigree reveals the history of your dog's family.

PUPPY TO CHAMPION

Ch. Snaefell Limited Edition

Five weeks: At this age you can get an idea of coat quality and markings, but the color is likely to change. The white tip to his tail will break the solid color on his back. The eyes need to be full and show no white, though this may improve. The muzzle needs to be short and square. A scissor bite will probably develop into the desirable undershot bite, as the lower jaw will grow on after the upper jaw.

Sixteen weeks: The teenage phase. The pup is teething and this affects many features, including the tail and the eyes. He may get snuffly and his nostrils may tighten. A youngster of this age often looks out of balance as both ends can grow at a different pace. It is worth waiting until teething is over to make a proper assessment.

Nine months: Teething is over, but he still has his puppy coat. However, you now have a very good idea of how he will turn out. Remember to take note of his movement, which should be free and striding. The front legs must not be bowed.

One year: The only change is that he now has his adult coat. Note how the white tail tip has grown long. The ears blend in with the head, and the top-knot has grown. This youngster was a Top Puppy winner in the breed in Britain.

A fully mature Champion, with 11 CCs, 4 Best of Breeds and 10 Reserve CCs to his credit. He has also sired a Champion daughter.

CHAPTER NINE

HEALTH CARE

**Trevor Turner
BVetMed, MRCVS**

The Shih Tzu is a native of Tibet, but was developed over centuries in China. The name in Chinese means Lion Dog and the Breed Standard, according to the Peking Kennel Club, calls for a "lion head, bear torso, camel hoof, feather duster tail, palm leaf ears, rice teeth, pearly petal tongue with movement like a goldfish." Perhaps centuries of having to fulfil such exacting criteria explains why this delightful little dog, happy to be part of any family, has relatively few problems specifically associated with the breed. However, not surprisingly, there are some eye problems particularly associated with the large, dark, round eye that is called for in the Kennel Club and American Kennel Club Standards.

None of these conditions have been shown to be inherited, thus the Shih Tzu is not specifically involved with any of the breeding eradication schemes. These, and other problems associated with the prominent eyes, are discussed later in this chapter.

PREVENTATIVE CARE

As soon as the veterinarian mentions "preventative care" to any owner of a new puppy, thoughts of vaccination and deworming immediately spring to mind. In fact, preventative medicine involves much more than this.

Breed Standards of the Shih Tzu all make reference to the sturdy, active, alert nature and the all-essential abundant coat, "luxurious, long and dense." This, together with the almost terrier-like, bouncy temperament and renowned adaptability of the breed, gives a clue to two other important areas of preventative care.

Firstly, if you decide to own this breed, you must also be fond of grooming or at least learn to like it, since there is not only a long flowing topcoat, but also a very dense undercoat which needs regular attention (see Chapter Five). This in itself has benefits extending beyond those for the dog. Grooming has an extraordinarily calming effect on the groomer, as well as being necessary to the recipient!

The other aspect of preventative care which can so easily be overlooked is the need for a good, balanced, controlled diet and regular exercise. Although classified as Toy dogs in the United States (Utility Group in Britain), Shih Tzus are anything but lap dogs. However, their innate adaptability, one of the endearing characteristics of the breed, will allow them to adjust to the role should necessity dictate. So, with an over-indulgent owner, tidbits and little exercise, this bouncy, outgoing extrovert can soon become a couch potato. Controlled tidbits are great as training rewards, but should never replace a well-balanced diet. (See Chapter Five.)

VACCINATION

Dogs, like people, can develop a natural immunity as the result of exposure to disease. For example, infectious tracheobronchitis (kennel cough) is extremely contagious but seldom life-threatening. It does cause a nasty, persistent, contagious cough which can be particularly persistent in brachycephalic (flat-faced) breeds, of which the Shih Tzu is one. In an otherwise healthy dog, full recovery can be expected and a strong immunity develops that will last for about six months.

The same principle applies to other diseases. Distemper is a considerably more serious disease than kennel cough and, before vaccination, was rife. Following natural infection, a number of dogs inevitably died, but those that survived had a solid immunity which was continuously reinforced by contact with other dogs carrying the virus, since it was so prevalent.

A few years ago, distemper was but one of several common canine killer diseases. Many dogs succumbed or were left with permanent disabilities, and it was for this reason that vaccines were developed.

Vaccination (inoculation) stimulates the dog to produce active immunity against one or, as is more popular today, a collection of diseases without developing any signs of that disease. The puppy acquires some immunity from the dam while in the womb. After birth, immunity is enhanced (boosted) all the time the puppy nurses. This is passive immunity. Once weaning takes place, this soon fades and that is when the puppy should receive primary vaccination to stimulate his own immunity. This will protect him just as natural immunity protected the dog that survived natural disease.

The immunity acquired from natural disease or primary vaccination does not last forever. Over the years, due to vaccination, many of these serious canine killer diseases are no longer rife, thus natural challenge does not occur. Therefore, regular boosters are required.

Inoculation and Vaccination

Strictly, inoculation means introducing an agent into the tissues of the body to stimulate an immune response. This usually involves an injection, but the human smallpox vaccine, for example, was introduced by scarifying the skin of the arm.

Vaccination similarly stimulates the subject to produce immunity against a disease without developing signs, but it need not necessarily be directly introduced into the tissues of the body. Thus, returning to kennel cough as an example, vaccination is achieved by instilling a few drops up the nose.

Vaccinations can begin as soon as natural immunity from the mother has waned.

Primary Vaccination

Primary vaccination should be started as soon as the passively-acquired immunity from the mother has declined sufficiently to allow the puppy to develop his own active immunity, otherwise circulating maternal antibodies destroy the vaccine and no immunity develops. When the passive immunity subsequently wanes, the puppy is totally unprotected.

Vaccination takes time to stimulate this active immunity and it is during this period that the puppy is vulnerable to infection. This immunity gap occurs at the same time as it is desirable to start introducing the puppy to as many new experiences as possible in order to ensure that he matures into a well-integrated family dog. Developing vaccines that will stimulate active immunity in the puppy, even in the face of circulating maternal antibodies, has been the goal of vaccine manufacturers for many years. Today, vaccines are available that can be started as early as six weeks, and give a solid protection by ten weeks of age.

The timing of vaccination and the vaccine used depends on disease prevalence in the area, together with other disease factors, as well as on the puppy. Call your local veterinarian and ask about vaccination policy. You can also discuss appointment details, prices and facilities and whether the practice organizes puppy classes or knows where these are available. These are socialization classes where your new Shih Tzu, bouncy, outgoing and full of infectious enthusiasm, will learn at least the fundamentals of rudimentary canine etiquette.

Booster Vaccinations

Vaccination shots do not last forever. It is for this reason that veterinarians advise regular boosters. The problem is, when and how frequently? Traditionally, veterinarians have recommended routine, annual, across-the-board boosting. Recently, boosters have become a matter of concern both for veterinarians and dog owners alike.

Polyvalent (multivalent) vaccines give protection against a collection of diseases. They are very popular and economical, costing considerably less (in terms of cash, time and stress) than separate injections against each of the inoculable diseases. However, recently, both their function and their safety has been questioned.

Veterinarians are advised to follow manufacturers' instructions with any drug, including vaccines. In order to obtain a product licence, vaccine manufacturers have to submit evidence regarding the safety and efficacy of any product. With a vaccine, this includes duration of immunity. The latter, due to cost and other factors, is usually looked at over 12 months, hence when a product licence is issued, provided there is no evidence of reaction or other safety issues on boosting immunity, a recommendation will be included for this to be reinforced after one year.

This procedure is presently under review by manufacturers. Some are suggesting that, with certain diseases (distemper and hepatitis for example), annual boosters may not be strictly necessary. Professionally, and this view is based on more than 40 years of busy canine practice, I have to say that the risk of reaction is so slight compared with the threat of disease in unprotected dogs that I would rather go for over-vaccination than to have to relive my personal experiences of major canine epidemics. However, if you have concerns, discuss them with your veterinarian at the time of primary vaccination. Your views will be respected and the risks and benefits for your particular pet, according to disease prevalence in your area, will be fully examined.

Measuring Immunity

Blood tests are available for both puppies and adult dogs which will indicate the dog's level of immunity for any of the diseases against which we normally vaccinate. From these results, your veterinarian can accurately advise whether there is a necessity for revaccination. However, be forewarned. It is likely that the cost of testing for each disease will be as much as a combined booster against all the diseases. Money apart, it

Discuss the subject of booster vaccinations with your vet.

is also arguable whether this blood testing is in the dog's best interest. Taking the sample from a Shih Tzu is not the easiest of tasks. Despite the fact that the sample is only a few drops, your dog will probably consider it far more stressful having to keep still for a few seconds in a strange position and environment than enduring a booster jab that can cover anything up to six diseases with one quick and simple injection.

Core and Non-Core Vaccines

The veterinary profession today acknowledges there are drawbacks associated with some vaccines. In consequence, there has been a move to divide vaccination into two groups, core vaccines and non-core vaccines.

Core (essential) vaccines are those that protect against diseases that are serious, fatal, or difficult to treat. In Britain, these include distemper, parvovirus, and adenovirus (hepatitis). In the United States, rabies is also included. With the current change in quarantine laws in Great Britain, rabies vaccine may well become a core

vaccine in that country in the not-too-distant future.

The vaccines considered less essential include bordetella, leptospirosis, coronavirus and borrelia (Lyme disease). This latter vaccine is used widely in North America and does cause reactions in a number of dogs. Lyme disease is caused by bacteria which are transmitted through the bites of the deer tick. It is relatively rare in the United Kingdom, although very common in certain parts of North America.

Contagious Diseases

Bordetellosis (also known as kennel cough or infectious tracheobronchitis), is not usually life-threatening except in very young and elderly dogs. The usual sign is a persistent cough. In Britain, *Bordetella bronchiseptica*, a bacterial organism, is considered the primary cause, with viruses implicated as secondaries. In the United States, parainfluenza virus is considered the main cause, with bordetella as a secondary invader.

Today, both in the United Kingdom and the United States, most multivalent vaccines include a parainfluenza component. The bordetella vaccine is administered separately via nasal drops which have been shown to give a better immunity than conventional vaccination by injection.

Recently introduced on both sides of the Atlantic is a combined parainfluenza and borde-tella vaccine, again in the form of nasal drops.

Canine distemper

In developed countries, such as the United States and Britain, canine distemper is no longer as widespread as previously. This is entirely due to preventative vaccination.

Signs (symptoms) vary. Fever, diarrhea, coughing, discharges from the nose and eyes are all seen. Sometimes the pads will harden, a sign of the so-called hardpad variant. Fits, chorea (twitching of groups of muscles) and paralysis can be seen in a high proportion of infected dogs. The virus can also be implicated in the so-called kennel cough syndrome.

Hepatitis

Canine hepatitis, perhaps better known in North America as adenovirus disease, can show signs ranging from sudden death with the peracute infection to mild cases where the patient is just a bit "off-color." Most cases present with fever, enlargement of all the lymph glands and a swollen liver. During recovery, the clear part of the eye (cornea) can become edematous (fluid-filled) and appear cloudy, thus the dog may look blind. This "blue eye" is very worrying for any owner but usually resolves quickly without impairing sight. Adenovirus is, again, a component of the kennel cough syndrome.

Canine Parvovirus, CPV

This is really new in that it effectively hit the canine population of the world in the 1980s. It is caused by a virus that can exist in the environment for a long time. Main signs include vomiting and diarrhea, often with blood present (dysentery).

Control of this disease is largely one of the unsung triumphs of modern veterinary medicine for it has been undoubtedly due to the rapid development of highly effective vaccines.

Rabies

Rabies is present on all continents except Australasia and Antarctica. Several countries, of which Britain is one, are free of the disease. The virus does not survive long outside the body. The disease is transmitted by wildlife, such as foxes, or, in some parts of the world, stray dogs. Transmission is mainly by biting. It is an extremely serious disease communicable to humans (zoonotic) which disrupts the central nervous system.

Vaccination using an inactivated (killed) vaccine is mandatory in many countries, including the United States. In Britain, it is not yet mandatory to have a dog vaccinated against rabies unless the owner wishes to travel to certain authorized countries and return to Britain under the PETS travel scheme.

Lyme Disease

This is a tick-borne bacterial disease, causing acute, often recurrent, polyarthritis in both dogs and humans. Fever, cardiac, kidney and neurological problems can occur in some cases. A vaccine is available in the United States.

Coronavirus Disease

Coronaviral gastro-enteritis occurs worldwide but the signs are milder than those of parvovirus. Younger dogs, 6 to 12 weeks old, appear to be more susceptible to this disease, and, in some kennels, 100 percent of the dogs may be affected. Spontaneous recovery occurs in 7 to 10 days, although diarrhea may persist for several weeks. There is no licensed vaccine available in Britain, although vaccines are available in America.

PARASITES

Routine parasite control is an important part of preventative care for any dog. This is particularly so in the case of ectoparasites, such as lice, fleas and ticks, in the abundantly-coated Shih Tzu where the opportunist lodger may well go undetected. However, this area of preventative care should also cover endoparasites. These include roundworms, tapeworms and hookworms together with heartworm, which is important in Southern Europe and North America.

ECTOPARASITES

Fleas

These are the most common ectoparasites found on dogs. Some dogs can carry very high flea burdens without showing any signs, whereas others will develop flea allergy dermatitis from being bitten only once or twice.

Fleas are not host-specific; both dog and cat fleas can be found on dogs, cats and humans.

The dog flea – Ctenocephalides canis.

Despite your care and vigilance, fleas can be picked up from urban gardens (yards) since hedgehogs, squirrels and racoons can all act as vectors. If the flea is in need of a blood meal, which is essential for the completion of its life cycle, we are just as likely to be bitten as our pets.

Effective flea control involves both the adult fleas on the dog and also immature stages which develop in the home environment. Having dined on the blood of the host, the female flea then commences egg laying. This may be on the dog, or, as is more likely, she will hop off to lay eggs in the environment. If laid on the dog, even a breed as full-coated as the Shih Tzu, the eggs soon drop off to develop in the carpets and crevices of the home.

Development depends upon the temperature and humidity and it can be as short as three weeks. Fleas can survive in suitable environments for more than a year without feeding. This is the reason why dogs, and people, can be bitten when entering properties left unoccupied for some time after previous pets have gone.

Flea Control

Control in the home should include thorough vacuuming to remove immature stages. The use of an insecticide with prolonged action to kill any developing fleas is also worthwhile. Few insecticides currently on the market kill flea larvae.

Treatment of your dog can take several forms: oral medications, which prevent completion of the life cycle of the flea; applications in the form

Dogs should be treated regularly for fleas.

of sprays, spot liquids, or powders; and insecticidal baths.

Bathing has little residual effect and therefore should be combined with other methods of flea control. Spot preparations are very popular. These use sophisticated technology to disperse the chemical over the invisible fat layer which covers the skin. The chemical does not actually enter the body. Within 24 hours of application, the dog will have total protection against fleas for approximately two months, and this protection will survive two or three routine baths. When a flea bites the dog, it has to penetrate through the fat layer to get to the blood and thus ingests the chemical.

Although many effective flea preparations are available over the counter from pet stores and supermarkets, it is, nevertheless, worthwhile discussing strategy with your veterinarian. Many of the longer-lasting, more effective compounds are available from veterinarians only. Also, your veterinarian will be much more aware of the flea problem in the locality and will be able to work out a control strategy with you.

Lice

Lice are not usually such a widespread problem as fleas. They do not live away from the host and therefore require direct contact for transmission. The eggs (nits) are attached to individual hairs. A lice-ridden dog is usually a very itchy dog, and careful examination of the coat usually reveals the culprits, or, at least, the nits stuck to the base of the hairs.

Ectoparasiticidal shampoos are effective. Bedding should be washed and sprayed with an appropriate ectoparasiticide.

Ticks

Ticks can be a problem in some areas, both in Britain and North America. They are important since they can be the carriers of various diseases that can affect your Shih Tzu. Lyme disease (particularly common in North America), *babesiosis*, and *ehrlichiosis* are examples. The two latter diseases are now important as far as Britain is concerned, due to the freedom of travel for pets to certain parts of Europe and other authorized countries under the PETS Travel Scheme without the need to undergo quarantine on return.

Some flea and louse preparations are also licensed for tick control. Some of the spot

Spot preparations are effective over a longer period of time.

preparations, in particular, have prolonged activity even if you bathe your dog several times between applications.

Harvest Mites

These can be a source of irritation to your Shih Tzu if he is normally exercised in fields and woodland locations in the autumn (fall) – particularly if there is a chalky subsoil. The feet and muzzle are most affected.

The parasite is the immature form (larva) of a mite that lives in decaying organic matter. The tiny red larvae are just visible to the naked eye, and cause intense irritation. Prolonged-action insecticidal sprays are effective in ridding your pet of the problem and preventing reinfestation.

Walking Dandruff (*Cheyletiellosis*)

This is an unusual condition in the Shih Tzu but can occasionally occur. The surface-living mite can just be seen with the naked eye, particularly along the back and, sometimes, underparts. There is always excess dandruff visible, in which

the mites will be found. Treatment with any of the ectoparasiticidal preparations results in rapid cure. Although rare, *Cheyletiellosis* is important because it is a zoonosis, affecting humans, particularly children.

ENDOPARASITES

Roundworms

Roundworms are virtually ubiquitous in puppies. There are several types, but the most common is *Toxocara canis* which is a large, round, white worm 3-6 inches (7-15 cm) long.

The life cycle is complex and includes migration through the tissues of the host. Larvae (immature worms) can remain dormant in the tissues for long periods. In the pregnant female, under hormonal influence, these dormant larvae can become activated and cross the placenta into the unborn puppy. There, they develop into adult worms in the small intestine, resulting in puppies, perhaps only ten days old, shedding infected roundworm eggs. Larvae are also passed from the mother to the puppy during suckling via the milk.

Veterinarians advise the regular worming of litters from approximately two weeks of age. Treatment should be repeated regularly until the puppy is at least six months old. Because there is a slight risk that humans can become infected, adult dogs should be routinely wormed about twice a year.

Effective preparations are available without prescription. Nevertheless, it is worthwhile discussing control with your veterinarian who

All puppies carry a burden of roundworm.

will be able to supply you with effective prescription preparations that cover a whole variety of worms with a single dose.

Adult dogs become reinfected from sniffing infected feces, but often show few signs. Heavily-infected puppies may show signs of malnutrition, despite the fact that they appear to be eating well. A variety of signs can occur, including a distended abdomen ("pot-belly"), diarrhea, vomiting, obstruction of the bowel and even death.

Tapeworms (Cestodes)

These are the other important class of worms found in the dog. Unlike roundworms, they have an indirect life cycle, meaning they cannot be spread from dog to dog directly, but must employ an intermediate host (such as fleas, sheep, horses, rodents and sometimes humans, depending on the type of tapeworm involved). The most common tapeworm of the dog (and cat), *Dipylidium caninum*, uses the flea as the intermediate host.

The mature worm lives in the intestine and can measure up to 20 inches (50 cm). Eggs are contained within mature segments which break off from the end of the worm and are passed in the feces. These sometimes can be seen looking like grains of rice stuck around the dog's anus. Free-living flea larvae swallow the tapeworm eggs which mature as the flea develops. Dogs then swallow infected fleas during normal grooming habits and so the life cycle is completed. Effective tapeworm treatments are available, but fleas must also be controlled if the problem is to be overcome.

Tapeworms are usually found in the adult dog, and, although it is aesthetically unpleasant to see tapeworm segments wriggling out of the anus, tapeworm infestation, unless very heavy, has surprisingly few effects on the normal healthy adult dog.

Heartworm

Dirofilaria immitis is a large worm, up to 11.5 inches (30 cm) in length. These worms inhabit the pulmonary artery and sometimes the right atrium of the heart, together with other parts of the circulatory system where they cause serious problems. The parasite is transmitted by mosquitoes and is prevalent in many parts of Southern Europe and the United States.

Effective prophylactic remedies are available to prevent the onset of heart failure, which, at one time, was only too commonly seen in infected dogs.

Hookworms, Whipworms And Lungworms

These worms can also cause problems in certain

Far from being a lap dog, the Shih Tzu is an energetic dog who can get up to all types of mischief.

areas. Your local veterinarian will advise if any special remedies or precautions have to be taken.

Other Endoparasites

Endoparasites do not only involve worms. *Coccidia*, *Giardia* and other single-celled organisms can cause problems, especially in kennels. Your local veterinarian will advise.

EMERGENCY CARE AND FIRST AID

Shih Tzus are, at heart, active extroverts and the unexpected is always just around the corner. Emergencies come in all forms, road accidents, bites, burns, heat stroke, insect stings, poisoning and collapse.

First aid is the initial treatment given in an emergency. The purpose is to preserve life, reduce pain and discomfort, and minimize any risk of permanent disability or disfigurement.

It is hoped that the following basic principles will help if you are faced with an emergency situation.

Priorities

Keep calm and try not to panic. If possible, get help. Contact your veterinarian, and explain the situation so he or she can give you specific first-aid advice, according to the situation.

If there is the possibility of internal injury, try to keep your dog as still as possible. With a Shih Tzu, this is easier than with some of the larger breeds of dog.

If the dog is in shock (see below), warmth is essential. A cardboard box will keep him warm, confined and reasonably still, and is useful for transportation. Use blankets, if available, or wrap up your Shih Tzu in a coat, or even newspaper.

Take your dog to the veterinarian as soon as possible. Drive carefully, observe the speed limits, and, if possible, take someone with you to keep an eye on the dog while you drive.

Shock

Shock is a complex condition that is difficult to define. Basically, it is due to a lack of fluid in the cells, tissues or organs, and results in a serious fall in blood pressure.

Causes include:
- Loss of blood due to injury
- Heart failure
- Acute allergic reactions.

First signs include:
- Rapid breathing and heart rate
- Pallor of the mucous membranes of the gums, lips or under the eyelids

- Feet or ears may feel cold to the touch
- Vomiting may occur
- The dog is often very quiet and unresponsive.

Dealing with shock should include the following measures:
- Try to conserve heat, cover with coats, blankets or even newspapers
- Keep quiet and in a dim light if possible
- Seek immediate veterinary help
- Apply the A, B, C of first aid if necessary (below).

If you know the basics of first aid, you will be able to care for your dog in any situation.

THE A, B, C OF FIRST AID

A	Airway
B	Breathing
C	Cardiac function

A=Airway

Injuries to the mouth or throat can happen when playing with a stick, and result in airway problems, vomiting, collapse or choking, which can obstruct breathing. Do your best to clear the mouth and throat in order to allow the passage of as much air (oxygen) to the lungs as possible.

Do not put your fingers in your Shih Tzu's mouth. Remember, your dog will be just as terrified as you are, and, if fighting for his life, may well bite in panic. Use any blunt object such as a piece of wood, or the back of a spoon, to try to open the mouth. Sometimes you can drop a loop of material (such as a tie or piece of string) around the upper and lower canine teeth and gently open the mouth that way.

B=Breathing

If your dog does not appear to be breathing, try gently pumping the chest with your hand, at the same time feeling just behind the elbow to try to detect a heartbeat (pulse). If not detected quickly, move on to cardiac massage (see below).

C=Cardiac Function

In a normal Shih Tzu, cardiac pulse can easily be felt by placing your hand around the sternum, just behind the front legs. If nothing can be felt, try gently squeezing the ribs in this area, 15 to 20 squeezes a minute, stopping every half minute or so to see if you can detect a heartbeat. This is sometimes successful in getting the heart beating again.

Check the color of the tongue; if cyanotic (blue), place a handkerchief over the mouth and nose, and try forcing your breath down the throat and nose.

EMERGENCIES

Bleeding

If hemorrhage is severe from a cut pad, a tight bandage can be applied using any available clean material. A polythene bag applied between the layers of bandage will keep the blood contained. The aim is to prevent as much blood loss as possible. Get your dog to the veterinarian as soon as possible. If you have bandaged the limb very tightly, make sure it is not left on for more than 15 or 20 minutes without rebandaging.

If bandaging is impractical, endeavor to control the bleeding by applying finger or hand pressure, preferably with a piece of clean dressing material between your hand and the wound.

Burns and Scalds

Cool the burned area with cold water as quickly as possible, and cover with damp towels. If the burn is due to a caustic substance, wash as much of this away as you can with plenty of cold water. If in the mouth, press cloths soaked in clean, cold water between the jaws.

Eye Injuries

The Breed Standard expects the Shih Tzu to have large, round eyes, and just such an eye can be injury-prone, whether due to foreign bodies (grass seeds) or scratches (cats' claws or bushes). Cover the eye with a pad soaked in cold water, or, better still, saline solution (contact lens solution) and seek veterinary help as soon as possible.

Fits and Seizures

Convulsions, fits or seizures are not common in the Shih Tzu, but they can occur following head injury. Although very frightening for the onlooker, the dog does not know what is happening.

If possible, place him in a dark, confined area where he cannot damage himself, touching him as little as possible. A cardboard packing case makes an ideal environment for a dog of this size. Most seizures only last a few seconds or minutes. It is better to wait until there has been some recovery before going to the veterinarian. If the seizure continues for more than three or four minutes, contact your veterinarian immediately.

Heatstroke

Heatstroke is the all-too-frequent result of dogs being left in cars with too little ventilation. The car need not be in direct sunlight to kill your dog. Body temperature rises rapidly and this soon results in irreversible damage. Signs are excessive panting with obvious distress. Unconsciousness and coma quickly follow.

Try to reduce body temperature by bathing the dog in copious amounts of cold water, then wrap the still-wet animal in damp towels and take him to the veterinarian as soon as possible.

BREED-SPECIFIC PROBLEMS

It seems that this "Little Lion Dog" has a constitution to match his name, since there are very few problems which can be specifically associated with the Shih Tzu.

The Shih Tzu is a hardy little dog, and suffers from few inherited disorders.

Eye Problems

There are several ophthalmic problems that are associated with a short-faced anatomy. Injuries to the large, round eye are not uncommon. Sometimes these are so slight that the only sign is that the eye is watering (tearing) excessively. In excessively sunny, windy or cold conditions, inflammation of the cornea or clear part of the eye, so-called exposure keratitis, can occur. This can lead to painful corneal ulceration.

Epiphora

"Wet eye" or epiphora is an abnormal overflow of tears. It is usually seen as staining of the hair down the face. It can be the result of exposure keratitis (mentioned above) or be due to poor drainage by the tear duct (nasolacrymal duct) due to the short face. This can be a major problem in some brachycephalic breeds but is not an inherent problem in the Shih Tzu. Other causes of epiphora are corneal ulceration and sometimes "dry eye" due to the loss of the protective tear film.

One common cause of wet eye in the Shih Tzu is irritation from the "shock" (the fringe which falls over the eyes), as described in the Breed Standard. An elastic hair tie, keeping the hair out of the eyes, is indispensible in the breed.

Other Eye Disorders

Occasionally, some Shih Tzus have an inturned lower eyelid (entropion), which can cause corneal irritation. This is not very common in the breed. Extra eyelashes (distichia), which rub on the eyeball, are also occasionally seen. Progressive retinal atrophy (PRA) is seen sometimes with the onset of middle age. Unlike the Lhasa Apso, a breed closely associated with the Shih Tzu (see Chapter One), there is no evidence that the condition is inherited in the Shih Tzu.

Breathing Problems

Many snub-nosed dogs do have breathing problems, but this is not a problem in the Shih Tzu. However, if unfortunate enough to contract any upper respiratory tract infection (URTI), breathing can become difficult. If there are any changes in breathing patterns, see your veterinarian sooner rather than later.

SUMMARY

Despite some of the problems described above, the Shih Tzu is generally a healthy dog, with a healthy appetite for life. Happy, loyal, comical, and affectionate, the Shih Tzu is a joy to share your life with.